Please remember that this is a library book,
and that it belongs only temporarily to each
person who uses it. Be considerate. Do
not write in this, or any, library book.

To hope

ADVANCES IN CONTEMPORARY EDUCATIONAL THOUGHT SERIES
Jonas F. Soltis, EDITOR

THINKING

THE FOUNDATION OF CRITICAL AND CREATIVE LEARNING IN THE CLASSROOM

Robert Boostrom

Teachers College, Columbia University
New York and London

Published by Teachers College Press, 1234 Amsterdam Avenue, New York, NY 10027

Library of Congress Cataloging-in-Publication Data

Boostrom, Robert E., 1949–
    Thinking: the foundation of critical and creative learning in the classroom / Robert Boostrom.
        p.   cm. — (Advances in contemporary educational thought series)
    Includes bibliographical references and index.
    ISBN 0-8077-4569-3 (cloth : alk. paper)
    1. Education—Philosophy.   2. Thought and thinking.   I. Title.   II. Series.

    LB14.7.B654 2005
    370.15'2—dc22   2004063781

ISBN 0-8077-4569-3 (cloth)

Printed on acid-free paper
Manufactured in the United States of America

12   11   10   09   08   07   06   05   8   7   6   5   4   3   2   1

Contents

Foreword

The subject of this book is thinking in the classroom. Old wine in new bottles? What's so new about the idea of promoting thinking in classrooms? How can the treatment of this age-old topic be an advance in educational thought? In this book, Boostrom deftly shapes an old topic in new ways and convinces us straight off that thinking about thinking, let alone teaching it, is far from as straightforward a task as most of us tend to imagine and so act.

The book itself is an adventure in thinking about thinking. Boostrom begins with a thoughtful examination of Bloom's taxonomy and Gardner's multiple intelligences and their effects on educators' thinking about how to teach thinking. The first paradox he exposes is that the more we seek to define and codify methods for teaching thinking, the more these things become procedures and templates for teachers and students to mindlessly follow rather than promoting thinking. He then sketches a history of the liberal arts tradition undergirded by a belief in the liberation of the mind. He examines the current model of contemporary liberal arts curriculum, pointing out how such subjects and disciplines are easily perceived as out there to be learned, thus making it hard to think of their teaching and learning as an engagement in thinking as opposed to the acquisition of already thought-out knowledge.

The next part of the book deals with the paradox of telling. Teachers must tell students things, but so often, the telling of subject matter results in the unexamined receiving of that matter rather than inviting thought about it. Boostrom uses the analogies of storytelling and show-and-tell as well as the contrasting views of traditionalists and progressive teaching to explore ways that pedagogical telling can be seen to either thwart or encourage thinking. He also examines the effect of teaching thinking given the pedagogical realities of current cultural literacy programs and reader response theories.

The last part of the book explores the paradox of believing. Beliefs are generally taken by most people to be unproven assertions, while truth statements or facts are grounded and thus have reason to be accepted as true. Boostrom argues that students and teachers find themselves in a dualistic frame of mind, which they share with most other people in the 21st century—some statements are facts and some are opinions, and clearly the process of education is to convey and receive fact, not opinion. However, the problem with fact, according to Boostrom, is that it marks the end of thinking. So it is hard to cultivate thinking when fact and truth are what education is about. He then explores the contrast between original thinking and plagiarism and asks what kinds of non-thinking contemporary schooling and the use of the Web encourage.

This is a book to ponder, to worry over. It is haunting in its conclusions regarding the nature of contemporary schooling and the political and social world in which we live. The reader will find it to be an adventure in thought.

Throughout the work Boostrom does two things that enrich and enhance his exploration of thinking in classrooms. He frequently draws on his own experiences with his own students and other real educational situations to serve as concrete examples to illustrate his major points. He also deftly draws on some of the best of John Dewey's thought on the matter, from such works as *How We Think*, *Art as Experience*, *Logic: The Theory of Inquiry*, and *Democracy and Education*. It is remarkable how old thought encourages and enriches many new ways to think about teaching thinking and avoiding nonthinking in classrooms. This book is, indeed, a welcome advance in contemporary educational thought.

Jonas F. Soltis
Series Editor

THINKING

Introduction

The lesson was taught by Robert Frost. When a road diverges, the traveler who chooses one path rejects the other.

In classrooms, paths constantly diverge. Teachers make hundreds of choices every day. Not choices between good methods and bad methods, the right things to teach and the wrong things. Teachers must choose some desired goals and actions and in so choosing, reject other desired goals and actions. The third-grade teacher who spends a week making sure that all her students know their multiplication facts cannot spend that same week helping students discover solutions to "real world" problems. The first-grade teacher who takes it as her primary goal to get all her students to learn word attack skills cannot take it as her primary goal to get her students to love books. The teacher of Spanish who spends the majority of each class in conversation with her students cannot spend the majority of each class having her students read Spanish. In every classroom some worthwhile activities go undone.

No educative goals would be disregarded if teaching were simply a matter of doing the "right thing" or choosing "what works." To see teaching from this technological perspective is to suppose that the classroom is something like a maze in which the one entrance point and the one exit point can only be connected by making a series of correct choices from the numerous diverging paths. But this vision of teaching and schooling depends upon the assumption that there exists a singular and perfectly agreed upon notion of what schools are supposed to accomplish (one exit point) and upon the equally doubtful assumption that what works one time for one student works all the time for all students (one entrance point).

Unfortunately for those who espouse the "what works" notion of schooling, our society wants schools to make students more creative and more obedient, more critical and more grounded in traditional values, more specialized

1

and more well rounded, more able to select the right answer on a standardized multiple-choice test and more able to think of alternative answers. On top of conflicting aims, schools must deal with diverse students, whose needs, interests, abilities, and backgrounds not only differ but also change over time. This maze can be entered or exited almost anywhere. As a result, debates and complaints about schooling flourish regardless of the conditions of schooling: There is always something that isn't being done. There is always a road not taken.

This confusion about the aims of schooling passes almost unnoticed, so keen are the public, legislators, candidates for public office, and even many educators on establishing higher and ever higher standards, to be assessed by more and ever more frequent tests. Educational disputes involving such issues as "whole language" reading instruction, bilingual instruction, "cultural literacy," charter schools, and vouchers are wrongly taken to be disputes about methods for reaching the apparently God-given standards, instead of what they are—disputes about what we think school is for. So entrenched in public discourse is the "what works" notion of schooling that it may seem impossible to imagine any alternative.

One of the aims of this book is to sketch a vision of teaching that remains when the what-works notion is abandoned. Without the assumption of agreed-upon "standards," is it possible to take any stand on what teachers should know and be able to do? Is there anything we all agree on if we don't agree on the ends of schooling?

Certainly we can agree on noneducational matters. We want our schools to do no harm. We want the school environment to provide physical safety. We want school officials to monitor student behavior—at least enough so that teachers and administrators know where students are and what they are doing. But setting aside these minimal expectations for student welfare, is there any *educational* perspective that is both universally shared and prescriptive about what teachers should know and be able to do?

I believe that there is at least one point of agreement. We—teachers, parents, legislators, school administrators, professors of education, even students—can agree about our dissatisfaction with classrooms in which students do not think about what they are doing. We do not want teachers to create mechanical, sterile classrooms. We do not want our children to spend their lives engaged in busy but meaningless activity. We can recognize our agreement because we can point to instances of schooling that no one defends.

Twenty-five years ago I worked as a remedial-reading teacher in a Dallas high school. One day, weeks into the school year, I was asked by a teacher to visit her classroom to observe a student who the teacher believed had a reading problem. When I appeared in the classroom that afternoon, I saw a girl laboriously copying a passage from her textbook—one letter at a time.

It was clear that she was not merely "functionally illiterate," but completely unable to decode the simplest written English. She could not read her own name.

Now, the intriguing part of this story is that only one of the girl's several teachers contacted me about her, and this only after more than 6 weeks of the school year had passed. How was this totally illiterate student getting by in her courses? The answer painfully illustrates how there can be classrooms without thinking.

She was a quiet girl, one who never made any trouble, and this may have made it easy for teachers to overlook her. But the real key to her success was that she did her work. She had discovered that when the assignment was to "read the chapter and answer the questions" (as it often was), what she needed to do was to find in the reading assignment the string of letters that made up the question. She would then copy the string of letters that followed the question-letters. Doing this satisfied her teachers.

This fully non-thinking approach to curriculum may seem to be an extreme case, involving a special student who was simply mis-placed, but years later I discovered that her story was not as unusual as I wanted to suppose. My middle-school-aged son was doing his history homework, identifying some important historical figures, when I asked him what he was doing.

"Identifying Thomas Jefferson," he said.

"Third president of the United States," I suggested.

"Nope."

"Writer of the Declaration of Independence."

"Nope."

"Founder of the University of Virginia?"

"Nope."

"I give up. Who was Thomas Jefferson?"

"Vice president under John Adams."

"OK," I agreed, "but how do you know that's the answer?"

"It's easy," he explained to me. "You find where *Thomas Jefferson* is in bold face in the chapter, and you write down what comes after it."

No one wants this non-thinking kind of teaching and learning to be what schoolwork is about. Even students who are successful at "doing school" wish for "more moments of satisfaction where they feel they truly deserve the praise they receive for the tasks they accomplish," where they find themselves engaged (Pope, 2001, p. 172). We all know what it means to work when our "heart is not in it" or when we are "just going through the motions." The problem is that while it's clear what *non-thinking* looks like, it's not at all clear what *thinking* looks like. Saying that we want students to think is not the answer to a question; it's the statement of the problem that I seek to explore in this book. How do we recognize, let alone create, classrooms in which students think, classrooms guided by the pursuit of what John Dewey called "reflective experience"?

One problem in dealing with this question is the inadequacy of language. To say that all the stakeholders in schooling want students to think is insufficient and misleading. Both the illiterate girl and the middle-school boy are—according to any reasonable definition—thinking. In fact, it could be argued that they have insightfully solved the problem of how to satisfy the teacher and have therefore demonstrated some practical skill in thinking. If the task of students is to satisfy the teacher, these two have demonstrated the results of a "reflective experience," so the schooling activities I've described should be perfectly acceptable. Of course, the activities are not acceptable, which suggests that the underlying complaint is not simply about an absence of cognitive activity, but involves some specification of the objects or qualities of thought that is not ordinarily included in definitions of the word *thinking*. The thinking sought in classrooms involves reflective engagement with and understanding of (though not necessarily agreement with) intended curriculum. My focus on "intended curriculum" doesn't mean I believe that, say, math teachers want students to think only about mathematics, much less only about problem 35 on page 116, but it does mean that when the class is dealing with problem 35, if the students are not thinking about that problem, the lesson results in what I have called non-thinking.

Labeling the lesson "non-thinking" says nothing about the worth of the students' activity. The student who, during math class, draws a cartoon panel or imagines a new design for a computer game may well be engaged in something worthwhile—very likely more worthwhile than the intended math lesson. But the aim of educators is to make *schooling* worthwhile, not to provide a setting for students to work entirely on their own. Good teachers do not want to design and supervise non-thinking lessons. They want their students to think, and the teacher's aim of getting students to think entails getting them to think about some explicitly chosen objects of reflection, which are manifested in the curriculum.

The aim of getting students to think also implies standards of procedure and achievement. Some instances of thinking are judged to be better than others. Teachers speak of teaching students to think more clearly, more deeply, more creatively, or more critically. Educational reformers have employed many different terms in their pursuit of thinking. *Engagement, higher-order thinking, constructivism, critical thinking, child-centered instruction, active learning, passionate learning, negative education, transformative teaching*, and *open education* are just some of the terms that have been used to put before readers the image of a classroom in which students think. Each term implies an answer to the question of how to avoid classrooms in which non-thinking prevails, but advocates of the answers implied by these terms are likely to disagree about what a given teacher ought to do, despite their willingness to agree about what a given teacher ought *not* to do. Even champions of a single term (consider, for example, *constructivism* or *critical thinking*) often find that they are championing different views of teaching and learning and different classroom practices (for example, see McPeck, 1990; Phillips, 2000). Against this backdrop of tangled conceptions, does it make sense to ask how to recognize or create classrooms in which students think?

This book is about why I believe it does make sense and about the kind of teaching that can result from pursuing this question. The book is organized around three commonplaces of teaching and learning: (1) Instruction is divided into levels and disciplines; (2) teachers tell students things; and (3) students are human beings who desire the certainty of cognitive closure. These commonplaces are unavoidable elements of teaching and learning, and each of them contributes, to the problem of non-thinking because each of these three commonplaces of teaching and learning contains within it a paradox.

In Part I, I look at the paradox of defining. Instruction occurs within bounded domains (spelling, American history, algebra), each of which is structured by its own set of rules and its own ways of knowing, with the implication that students don't need to think, because they can simply follow the procedures of the discipline.

In Part II, I look at the paradox of telling. A teacher tells students things and through this telling seems to be saying that the students don't need to think, because they will be told what they need to know.

In Part III, I look at the paradox of believing. Students are human beings whose thinking is permeated with desires, opinions, and values, and they understandably ask why they need to think when they know what they believe.

What follows, in these three parts, is not an attempt to redefine thinking. It is not even an exhaustive treatment of the causes of non-thinking. But I hope it engages readers, as I have been engaged, to think about the ways in which the practice of teaching unconsciously promotes non-thinking. And I hope it persuades readers that it is more important for a teacher to be alert to occurrences of non-thinking than it is for her to guide her students toward a watered-down version of thinking.

PART I

The Paradox of Defining

CHAPTER 1

Categories of Thinking

S tudents study subjects.
This commonplace of schooling shows its effects even on young children who early on discover that there are parts of the school day (perhaps "music" or "P.E.") that they like and other parts of the day (perhaps "arithmetic" or "reading") that they would be happy to do without. Later in their school careers (a phrase that also shows the influence of subject, for the "career" is thought of as consisting of or drawing upon certain subjects), children often become students who are informally identified in terms of subjects. Noddings, for example, speaks of high school students who are part of the "art room crowd" or part of the "math office bunch" (1992, p. 160). And if the students continue their formal education long enough, they will be formally identified by the subject to which they belong, becoming a "major" in biology or English or elementary education. In fact, it might be said that one of the essential functions of schooling is to apprentice the child into those subjects that are congenial and likely to play an important part in the life of the adult.

Habits of mind—ways of thinking—are bred into students with their apprenticeship in a subject, and at times thinking seems to be the same as knowing a subject well. In George Eliot's novel *Middlemarch*, Dr. Lydgate complains about the practice of having a lawyer preside at a postmortem inquest:

> "People talk about evidence as if it could really be weighed in scales by a blind Justice. No man can judge what is good evidence on any particular subject, unless he knows that subject well. A lawyer is no better than an old woman at a *post-mortem* examination. How is he to know the action of a poison? You might as well say that scanning verse will teach you to scan the potato crops." (1872/1964, p. 155)

From Lydgate's point of view, thinking about a cause of death is not something for which lawyers have been equipped; they have studied the wrong subjects. Judging evidence is not (Lydgate is saying) a "thinking skill" that transcends fields of study, because there is no such thing as evidence-in-general or judging-in-general, only particular sorts of evidence judged to be fitting and convincing by the procedural standards of particular subjects.

Of course, there are problems with supposing that thinking is merely a matter of knowing a subject well, not the least of which being that this supposition segments experience and denies the unity of the lives we lead. "All studies," says John Dewey,

> arise from aspects of the one earth and the one life lived upon it. We do not have a series of stratified earths, one of which is mathematical, another physical, another historical, and so on. We should not be able to live very long in any one taken by itself. We live in a world where all sides are bound together. All studies grow out of relations in the one great common world. (1902/ 1990, p. 91)

Dewey would take issue with Lydgate, arguing that a death—the end of a human life—cannot be understood simply in terms of the action of a poison on isolated portions of anatomy. If we live in "one great common world," the subjects that we study cannot exist separately one from the other, and the thinking that we do must transcend the boundaries of subjects.

Here is the first paradox of thinking in classrooms: Students study subjects, and their thinking (within this instruction) is ineluctably about something in particular and necessarily shaped by that something; yet we know that somehow these subjects do not merely coexist but actually interpenetrate in "one great common world" and that instruction that is subject-bound does not explain thinking that must occur between those carefully maintained boundaries.

In this chapter and the following, I deal with the problem of defining curriculum and the effects of this defining on thinking and non-thinking. In Chapter 2 I will turn to the emergence of the concept of a "discipline." In this chapter I begin with the subject of thinking itself, and more specifically with this assertion: Attempts to clarify and define the concept of thinking almost inevitably diminish our grasp of thinking. The harder we try to nail down thinking, the more it eludes us. Why this should be so and how this dilemma influences non-thinking in schools are the issues I will ponder.

THE NATURE OF THINKING

Of all the activities in which human beings engage, the one that has historically been most closely associated with the essence of being human is thinking. Aristotle saw rationality as the distinguishing feature that set off the human soul from those of other (presumably lower) forms of life, and the Genesis account of creation (chapter 2) makes Adam's ability to think of names for "every living creature" a significant aspect of his dominion over them. This view of thinking "as a sort of gift, specially presented to man [sic], and the most important and decisive of all the differences which distinguish man from the other animals" of course underwent revision in the preceding century. Fifty years ago, Sir Frederic Charles Bartlett said flatly, "No serious and informed person can any longer accept this as the correct view" (1958, p. 11).

The modern change in attitude toward the role of thinking in human life and in the lives of other creatures reflects increasing interest in understanding thinking as a biological process. From the perspective of the neuroscientist, human thought may be more complex or subtle than that of a chimpanzee or a rat, but the difference is merely a matter of complexity, not of fundamental nature. Thinking is seen in terms of molecular processes that can be studied in any structured group of neural cells.

The advantages of this view (for what in educational writing is called "brain research," for example) are clear, but so are the limitations. Jean-Pierre Changeux writes:

> As a molecular biologist I find myself confronted with a formidable problem: how to discover the relationship between these elementary molecular building blocks [of the brain] and highly integrated functions such as the perception of beauty and scientific creativity. (Changeux & Ricoeur, 2000, p. 3)

Without rejecting the insights of molecular biology in a futile attempt to return to the view that thinking is "a sort of gift, specially presented to man," Changeux touches upon the deeper mystery. The act of thinking may be a biological process that links humanity with other creatures (rather than separating us from them), but it also has something of the gods in it. The quality of experience enabled by thought extends our sensibilities beyond the moment and beyond ourselves. In Dewey's language, the activity of reflective thought is an interaction that changes the environment as much as it does the thinker.

If the enigmatic origins of thinking were not enough to obscure the topic, the difficulties of analyzing the process of thinking are compounded by a logistical problem: The tool that we use is also the subject of our investigation. The scholar's approach to difficulties of this sort is typically to clear the terrain by carefully defining the terms or limiting the phenomena to be discussed. For example, John Dewey begins *How We Think* by observing that the use of the words *thinking* and *thought* is "so profuse and varied . . . that it is not easy to define just what we mean by them."

The aim of his first chapter becomes, then, "to find a single consistent meaning." He goes on to explore "four senses" of the words *thinking* and *thought*, moving from the broadest use ("everything that comes to mind") to a more restricted use ("only such things as we do not directly see, hear, smell, or taste"), to the most restricted use of the terms ("beliefs that rest upon some kind of evidence or testimony"). This final restriction of the terms has "two degrees," because in some cases a belief may be accepted "with slight or almost no attempt to state the grounds that support it," while in other cases the basis for the belief "is deliberately sought and its adequacy to support the belief examined." This final sense of *thinking* and *thought* is, Dewey says, thinking in its "eulogistic and emphatic" sense (1910/1991, pp. 1–2, 5). It is this sort of thinking—or "reflective thought"— that Dewey explores in his book, and with this in mind he is ready to define his topic:

> Thinking, for the purposes of this inquiry, is defined accordingly as *that operation in which present facts suggest other facts (or truths) in such a way as to induce belief in the latter upon the ground or warrant of the former* [italics in original]. (pp. 8–9)

Later in the book Dewey reinforces this position, and, speaking of what he calls "the central function of all reflection," he notes that "for one thing to *mean, signify, betoken, indicate,* or *point to* another" is "the essential mark of thinking" (p. 116).

Sir Frederick Charles Bartlett, in his book *Thinking*, goes through a similar process to define his terms. "It will be abundantly plain," he says, "that I am using the term 'thinking' in a more restricted technical sense than is convenient in everyday conversation." People use *thinking*, he notes, when they mean "any mental process that runs beyond immediate perception." It can refer to anything "occurring to mind," to forgetting and remembering, to believing, to certainty or the lack of it. The one and only common element in this process, says Bartlett, is that "there is something in all of them which cannot be wholly accounted for in terms of a response to an immediate external environment" (1958, p. 72). This leads Bartlett to his definition. Thinking, he says, "in my use of the word . . . is the use of information about something present, to get somewhere else" (p. 74).

Now, my question at this point is this: Are Dewey and Bartlett talking about the same thing?

Both are using the same words—*thinking* and *thought*—but both also agree that the topic is obscured by a lack of agreement about what these words mean. They both feel that to make any progress in such a study, one needs to pin down what sorts of phenomena the key terms are talking about, and both describe instances in which the key terms are used. The instances sound much the same: Dewey begins with "everything that comes to mind," while Bartlett begins with anything "occurring to mind." Dewey moves to "such things as we do not directly see, hear, smell, or taste," and Bartlett mentions "any mental process that runs beyond immediate perception."

Once they have established the multiplicity of meanings attached to *thinking* and *thought*, each offers his definition. In both definitions there is the sense that thinking involves a "pointing toward," and yet—despite all the similarities so far—the essential element of the definitions is not the same. While Dewey claims to have found the "best" sense of *thinking* in the achievement of adequately supported belief, Bartlett finds essential the role of originality or discovery in thinking, a quality he sees as the thread that links all the common uses of the terms *thinking* and *thought*.

Without the criterion of adequately supported belief in his definition, Dewey defines *thinking* much the same as Bartlett does, so it would be possible to argue that the discrepancy between the definitions comes from difference of purpose. Dewey wants to define one sense of *thinking* (so he adds the criterion of belief), while Bartlett wants to show what all the senses of *thinking* have in common. The problem with this argument is that Dewey's definition implies that many of the common uses of the term *thinking* (the ones he's not defining) are really not thinking at all. For Dewey, taking the criterion of adequately supported belief out of his definition is not a minor matter. It means that one is no longer thinking about *thinking*.

So, are Dewey and Bartlett talking about the same thing or not?

The difficulty in answering this question arises, I believe, because the nature of the overarching topic—"thinking"—is not addressed by the scholarly analyses made by Dewey and Bartlett. When scholars draw from a large topic (such as "thinking") smaller subtopics (Dewey's "reflective thinking" or Bartlett's "adventurous thinking"), the effort to make the large topic manageable succeeds by creating a subject of study that is intelligible on its own. That is, what Dewey says about "reflective thinking" and what Bartlett says about "adventurous thinking" isn't intended to inform readers about a more encompassing notion of thinking (if there is one).

The difficulty I have in mind can be illustrated by an example from another field of study. In his magnum opus, *A Study of History*, Arnold Toynbee argues that attempts to make history more manageable and intelligible through studying national states had failed because these national states are "fragments of something larger." An "intelligible field of historical study" cannot, he says, focus on anything smaller in scale than an entire civilization.

"The history of the United States, for instance, or the history of Britain, is
. . . a fragment of the history of Western Christendom or the Western Christian World" (1962, p. iii).

Most historians since Toynbee have not been persuaded by his argument,
and while they may have many reasons for dismissing him, I suspect that
one of the most potent reasons is an unwillingness to grant that there is any
such thing as "the history of Western Christendom." There are many histories and many interpretations of what "Western Christendom" denotes.
Toynbee's position (that a piece only makes sense in terms of the whole)
collapses if the existence or nature of the whole is itself in doubt. If "Western Christendom" is not a reality, but rather a term of convenience defined
differently by different writers, it cannot serve as a frame within which constituent parts must be studied if they are to be intelligible.

So, what is the status of *thinking*? Is it a term of convenience, with
vaguely understood boundaries, containing within it a variety of processes,
some of them closely allied, some only somewhat related, some not related
at all? Or does the word identify a definable set of activities, processes, and
skills, or perhaps a definable form of experience?

How these questions are answered determines how we view competing
assertions about the essential nature of thinking. If Dewey and Bartlett are
talking about different topics, they are not characterizing "thinking" at all,
and differences between them do not need to be reconciled. But if what they
say must be understood as contributing to a unified concept, differences
become problems to be explained.

Now, my purpose to this point has not been to establish a definition
of thinking, but to show (in an admittedly sketchy manner) that the nature
of thinking and thought is so far from certain that to venture such a definition serves chiefly to confuse the topic. The main work of this chapter is
now to show why it is unlikely for the uncertainty of thinking to find its
way into classroom discussions of thinking or into the curriculum for those
who are preparing to become teachers, and further, how it is that when
we suppose we know what we are talking about when we use the words
thinking and *thought*, we undermine the pursuit of thinking and encourage non-thinking.

CRITICAL THINKING

One of the most common moves that educators make in the attempt to clarify
the topic of thinking is to talk about "critical thinking." This change in terminology serves two purposes because not only does it seem to put the discussion on firmer footing than it would be by simply talking about "thinking"

but also it focuses attention on an aspect of thinking deemed especially significant for educators.

To illustrate how attempts to refine the concept of thinking by focusing on "critical thinking" can actually encourage non-thinking, I want to look at the experience of a university in the midwestern United States. While this is only one case, the events are not unique and probably parallel similar events that universities across the country experience when they design (or redesign) general-education programs.

At this university—let's call it Midwestern U.—the general education program was (over a period of years) substantially redesigned. Five categories of student development were defined, and faculty members were then encouraged to create courses for each category that would lead to the outcomes and goals defined for that category. One of the goals of the first category was the promotion of critical thinking, defined as "the ability to analyze and critically evaluate information."

The implementation of the new general-education program was quite successful, with many courses being nominated and accepted for all the categories—except for the critical thinking category. The council overseeing the admission of courses to the general-education program invariably became embroiled in bitter disputes whenever a "critical thinking" course was proposed. Courses could easily be reviewed for, say, the science category or the arts category, but few courses proposed for "critical thinking" escaped lengthy debate, leading usually to the course in question being denied admission to the general education program.

What accounts for this inability to agree about what exactly constitutes a "critical thinking" course? It might be attributed to the obstructive tendencies of a few contrary faculty members, except that the membership of the council changed from year to year, and the debates continued over a period of some 5 years. In fact, the problem lay not in the constitution of the council but in the nature of the category. "Critical thinking" proved to be no clearer a concept than mere "thinking" would have been.

While there are undoubtedly those who would conclude that this failure to recognize the attributes of a critical thinking course shows only that the faculty members of Midwestern U. had not read enough on the subject, I am not convinced that any level of research would have solved the problem. To explain this assertion I want to discuss the results of an informal survey I have given to a variety of groups, including attendees to two conferences (one a session at an annual meeting of the American Educational Research Association, the other a session at an annual meeting of the Association for General and Liberal Studies), several groups of K–12 teachers, and the members of a teacher education department at an East Coast university. The items in this survey come from discussions at Midwestern U. Some items represent positions taken by faculty members explaining why they felt a proposed course would or would not meet the requirements of a critical thinking course. Other items are versions of official university statements about critical thinking. Here is the survey:

Read the following statements and decide for each one if you agree or disagree. Write *A* or *D* in the blank.

_____ 1. Not every course or classroom activity is a *critical thinking* course or activity.

_____ 2. A *critical thinking* course should enroll no more than 35 students (and probably fewer than that).

_____ 3. To teach *critical thinking* is to deal with a specific subject matter or body of content material that is distinct from the traditional disciplines.

_____ 4. A *critical thinking* course should treat a few subjects in depth rather than surveying a field or covering a body of introductory material.

_____ 5. *Critical thinking* can only be taught to students of a certain minimum age or development.

_____ 6. Teaching *critical thinking* requires using certain pedagogical strategies.

_____ 7. *Critical thinking* refers to the examination or application of a method of analysis.

_____ 8. In general, students do not exhibit genuine *critical thinking*.

_____ 9. A *critical thinking* course requires substantial student activity and cannot be conducted primarily through lectures.

_____ 10. *Critical thinking* refers to reflection upon the processes or products of cognition in order to assess or evaluate results.

_____ 11. *Critical thinking* is a merely honorific term.

_____ 12. The meaning of *critical thinking* depends on the discipline within which the thinking is being done.

_____ 13. *Critical thinking* refers to the discussion or application of multiple forms of intelligence (aesthetic, moral, intrapersonal, kinesthetic, and so on).

_____ 14. Students in my classes are required to think critically.

_____ 15. *Critical thinking* is the scientific method.

_____ 16. To promote *critical thinking*, assignments and assessments must be open-ended.

_____ 17. *Critical thinking* is the ability to analyze and evaluate information.

_____ 18. *Critical thinking* refers to the application of "higher order" cognitive skills such as interpreting, synthesizing, applying, illustrating, inferring, comparing-contrasting, distinguishing the central from the peripheral, and predicting.

The responses to this survey were largely the same regardless of the group being surveyed. It didn't matter whether the respondents were K–12 teachers or professors at research universities, whether they identified themselves with a general-education program or a field of specialization, whether they came from different institutions or the same institution. All the groups responded along the same lines, which is to say that their responses split about evenly between *agree* and *disagree* on all the items except 8, 14, and 18.

In every group of respondents, there were those willing to argue that every course or classroom activity involves (or perhaps should involve) critical thinking, just as there were those willing to argue that *critical thinking* is a merely honorific term. In every group of respondents there were those willing to argue that lectures could engender critical thinking as easily as any other activity, just as there were those who remained convinced that only certain, nonlecture activities could result in critical thinking. In every group of respondents there were those willing to argue that critical thinking must involve reflection upon instances of thinking, just as there were those who insisted that critical thinking is, in fact, identical with scientific method.

At first glance, these results may seem to be entirely negative, proving only that in every group I surveyed there were a lot of people who didn't know anything about critical thinking. But I believe that there is a different lesson to be learned, one that becomes clearer through examination of the three items about which all the groups agreed.

The responses to items 8 and 14 present a curious contradiction. All the groups were nearly unanimous both that students do not exhibit critical thinking and that they themselves require their students to think critically. (The single exception was a group of students who affirmed that students *do*, in fact, exhibit critical thinking.) Now, if all teachers—regardless of what they are teaching and whether they are dealing with elementary or with graduate students—say they require their students to think critically, but these same teachers observe that students do not exhibit this behavior, what are the teachers telling us about critical thinking? What conclusions can be drawn from this apparent contradiction?

Several interpretations are possible. It may be that critical thinking is not teachable, so that no amount of teacher instruction and encouragement is going to change much what students do. Or it may be that critical thinking is hard work and unlikely to be exhibited by students unless they are being closely supervised and possibly coerced. Or it may be that teachers use the same language—"critical thinking"—to refer to a large range of behaviors, so that the thinking-behavior that Teacher A encourages is not what Teacher

B is trying to get students to do. Or it may be that an honorific sense of *critical thinking* is so closely identified with the role of the teacher that seeing oneself as a teacher is the same as seeing oneself as teaching critical thinking—without necessarily attaching any specific content to the concept of critical thinking. And from the point of view of the teacher, it's even possible that she sees herself as dedicated to a task that her colleagues have let slide or have abandoned altogether.

Other interpretations could undoubtedly be offered, but this brief list adequately demonstrates the underlying problem. As long as teachers are convinced both that they require their students to think critically and that students in general do not think critically, questions arise about the possibility of ever teaching students habits of critical thought. The nature—even the existence of the alleged educational outcome—is brought into doubt.

The unanimity of response to item 18 makes even more evident how serious the problem is. If the respondents agree that item 18 encapsulates the processes, practices, and skills that make up critical thinking, how can the diversity of responses to almost all the other items be accounted for? If teachers agree that synthesizing, applying, and illustrating are forms of critical thinking, how can there still be such disagreement about what critical thinking is and about what it requires?

Lauren Resnick's discussion of "higher-order thinking" suggests one answer to these questions. Admittedly, "higher-order thinking" may not be the same thing as "critical thinking" (although some people say that it is—see item 18 in my quiz), but Resnick's discussion points toward a way in which thinking (critical, higher order, reflective, adventurous—however we wish to characterize it) can resist definition but still seem familiar and identifiable. Resnick says, "[I]t is relatively easy to list some key features of higher order thinking. When we do this, we become aware that, although we cannot define it exactly, we can recognize higher order thinking when it occurs" (1987, pp. 2–3). What we recognize (according to Resnick) are not categories or forms of higher-order thinking, but characteristics, such as that it is nonalgorithmic and complex and that it involves nuanced judgment and uncertainty (p. 3).

The interesting thing about these characteristics is that they don't tell us what thinking is; they tell us what it is not. Thinking is not the operation of an algorithm; the "path" of thinking is "not visible" from a "single vantage point" (which is how Resnick explains what she means by "complex"); it is not a mechanical procedure (unlike "judgment," which is often used as a synonym for *thinking*); it is not certain. When we define thinking in terms of its uncertainty, its tentativeness, its incompleteness, or our inability to predict its ends or procedures, we ought to acknowledge that we are talking about what thinking is not. All too often, we enumerate the ways in which thinking eludes our attempts to pin it down, and then we pat ourselves on the back for having characterized so insightfully what thinking is. What is truly easy to recognize is non-thinking, because non-thinking is algorithmic, "visible," mechanical, and predictable.

The enigmatic nature of thinking is not resolved into clarity through replacing the term *thinking* with *critical thinking*, or with *higher-order thinking* or *synthesizing, applying, and illustrating*, or any of the other categories of thought. Analyses of the levels and domains of thinking—ways of segmenting curricula—undoubtedly add to our appreciation of the complexity of thought, but they do not eliminate the puzzle at the heart of thinking. "Let us be honest with ourselves," says Heidegger,

> the essential nature of thinking, the essential origin of thinking, the essential possibilities of thinking that are comprehended in that origin—they are all strange to us, and by that very fact they are what gives us food for thought before all else and always. (1968, p. 45)

We will find the "real nature of thought," according to Heidegger, "if only we will not insist, confused by logic, that we already know perfectly well what thinking is" (p. 45).

The problem for teachers, of course, is that they must behave as if they know what thinking is. Thinking—especially critical thinking—is what they are supposed to require of their students. In the classroom, *thinking* becomes a taken-for-granted term parsed into fixed levels and domains. I turn next to an examination of how these analyses of thinking as levels and domains encourage non-thinking.

LEVELS OF THINKING

Chances are that when most teachers encounter the phrase *levels of thinking*, they interpret it (more or less) in the terms defined by Bloom and colleagues' (1956) *Taxonomy of Educational Objectives: The Classification of Educational Goals (Handbook I: Cognitive Domain)*. This book is, in the words of the editors of a 40-year retrospective on the work, "arguably, one of the most influential educational monographs of the past half century" (Anderson & Sosniak, 1994, p. vii). Although the *Taxonomy's* influence can be measured by references to it in the work of other scholars (Anderson and Sosniak found "more than 150 citations to the *Handbook*" in the 1992 *Social Science Citation Index*), the more profound impact lies in the infusion of the work into the educational consciousness. Anderson and Sosniak relate what happened when "approximately 200 administrators and teachers" at a meeting were asked how many had heard of Bloom's *Taxonomy*: "Virtually every hand in the audience was raised" (p. vii).

This was not, however, the outcome that Bloom and his fellow writers had anticipated. They saw the *Taxonomy* as "a small volume developed to assist college and university examiners." Instead, it "has been transformed into a basic reference for educators worldwide." Bloom explains this "phenomenal growth . . . by the fact that it filled a void; it met a previously unmet need for basic, fundamental planning in education." Because educators were now able "to evaluate the learning of students systematically . . . they became aware that too much emphasis was being placed on the lowest level of the *Taxonomy*—'Knowledge.'" With the guidance of the *Taxonomy*, educators realized, says Bloom, that more time needed to be spent "on the higher mental processes that would enable students to apply their knowledge creatively," a realization that has deepened in significance "with the explosion of knowledge that has taken place during the past forty years." Writing in 1994, Bloom concludes that "the ability to use higher mental processes has assumed prime importance" (1994, 1).

Bloom's conclusion may seem to contradict the premise with which I began this book—namely, that non-thinking, not "higher mental processes," is the norm of school life. But Bloom isn't necessarily arguing that school life is dominated by higher mental processing, only that it should be. Regardless of what goes on in classrooms, the ideal of higher mental processes (or higher-order thinking) remains the holy grail of teaching, frequently elaborated by Bloom's claim that the "explosion of knowledge" compels teachers to embrace this pursuit.

To assess the claims of educational benefit made on behalf of Bloom's *Taxonomy*, I want to look more closely at how the *Taxonomy* classifies processes of thinking. Later I will be looking at the effects of this classification on non-thinking.

The first issue, as Bloom and colleagues say, is to "be clear what it is that is to be classified" (1956, p. 11). Although they were working with test materials, they did not claim to be classifying test items, because of the "unlimited number of ways" in which such materials might be classified. Instead they saw their work as "a classification of the student behaviors which represent the intended outcomes of the educational process." If all three volumes—psychomotor, cognitive, and affective—of the intended project had been completed, the Bloom team would have classified "the ways in which individuals are to act, think, or feel as a result of participating in some unit of instruction." But in 1956 only the "cognitive" volume had been completed, and it is "only such of these intended behaviors as are related to mental acts or thinking" that make up what is now commonly known as the Bloom *Taxonomy* (p. 12).

There are, of course, six categories in the *Taxonomy*—Knowledge, Comprehension, Application, Analysis, Synthesis, and Evaluation—which Bloom et al. subdivided into 20 subcategories (though Application has no subcategories). The teachers with whom I have worked for the past 10 years have almost all been aware of the Bloom *Taxonomy* and familiar with its six categories. In their classrooms many have displayed posters depicting or discussing the *Taxonomy*, and I have never encountered a teacher who questioned the desirability of fostering higher-order thinking or the use of higher mental processes.

My students have been so thoroughly familiar with Bloom's *Taxonomy*, in fact, that they have tended to dismiss as unnecessary my occasional efforts to discuss it. They know the categories and generally feel that the labels are self-explanatory (although I have yet to encounter among my students a teacher who was familiar with the subdivisions of the categories). In an effort to promote discussion, I have often given students a quiz calling for them to identify into which taxonomic category each of several test questions would be placed by Bloom. The items in the quizzes have usually been from the Bloom et al. book.

None of my students has ever been able to classify all the test items as Bloom et al. do. Rarely do students correctly classify even half the items. My students almost invariably place a test item into a higher category than that identified by Bloom et al. For example, items that (according to Bloom et al.) require students to engage in the behaviors associated with "Comprehension" are frequently labeled by my students as "Synthesis" or "Evaluation."

Given the pervasiveness of Bloom's *Taxonomy*, this inability to categorize items according to the scheme of the *Taxonomy* is puzzling. After all, "the major purpose in constructing a taxonomy of educational objectives is to facilitate communication" (Bloom et al. 1956, p. 10). That is, the *Taxonomy* was constructed precisely to make it possible for educators to agree about what sort of behaviors a test item required of students. The *Taxonomy* was supposed to be "an aid in developing a precise definition and classification of such vaguely defined terms as 'thinking' and 'problem solving'" (p. 10). It was supposed to make *thinking* a manageable term by dividing it into elements everyone could recognize and about which everyone could agree.

What went wrong?

The answer lies, I believe, in the elegant manner in which the *Taxonomy* (perhaps unintentionally) hit upon a deep truth about thinking. While Bloom attributed the "phenomenal growth" of the *Taxonomy*'s influence to a "need for basic, fundamental planning in education," I find a different need being met. To explain what I have in mind, I want to turn from how Bloom has described the *Taxonomy* to how others have made use of it.

An online search for the phrase "Bloom's taxonomy" returns dozens of sites that provide a summary of the *Taxonomy*. Many of these give brief definitions of the categories, along with a list of words associated with each category. Here, for example, are the "Analysis" definitions from two Web sites (selected randomly):

> The breaking down of informational materials into their component parts, examining (and trying to understand the organizational structure of) such information to develop divergent conclusions by identifying motives or causes, making inferences, and/or finding evidence to support generalizations. (Krumme, 1995)

> Examining and breaking information into parts by identifying motives or causes; making inferences and finding evidence to support generalizations. (Fowler, 1996)

A quick read shows that the second definition is merely an abbreviated version of the first—in the second, concerns about "organizational structure" and "divergent conclusions" have been left out—and it might be supposed that the authors at both sites substantially agree about what sort of thinking behaviors are indicated by the term *analysis*. But this supposition is brought into question by what follows the two definitions: two lists of words identifying the behaviors associated with "analysis."

> Breaks down; correlates; diagrams; differentiates; discriminates; distinguishes; focuses; illustrates; infers; limits; outlines; points out; prioritizes; recognizes; separates; subdivides. (Krumme, 1995)

> Analyze, categorize, classify, compare, contrast, discover, dissect, divide, examine, inspect, simplify, survey, take part in, test for, distinguish, list, distinction, theme, relationships, function, motive, inference, assumption, conclusion. (Fowler, 1996)

Just two words—*distinguish(es)* and *infers/inference*—appear on both lists, but this obvious lack of congruity only begins to suggest the problem. Would the author of the second list accept *outlines* from the first list? Would the author of the first list accept *list* from the second list? If not, what principles guide the selection of terms for the two lists, and why are these principles different? And the problem is worse if both authors decide to adopt all the terms from the other list, for then it begins to seem as if any act of thought becomes "analysis."

The boundaries of analysis are further blurred by a list of question-starters that the author at the second Web site provides. Here are some of the questions designed to elicit the behaviors associated with analysis:

> What are the parts or features of . . . ?
> How is _____ related to . . . ?
> Why do you think . . . ?
> What is the theme . . . ?
> What motive is there . . . ?
> What ideas justify . . . ? (Fowler, 1996)

Now, I don't know that Bloom would have argued that some of these question-starters are inconsistent with analysis, but I suspect he would have been concerned about the potential for confusion that arises when teachers assume that questions phrased in certain ways necessarily elicit certain kinds of thinking. Analysis is not a kind of question; it's a kind of thinking, one that shades off, says Bloom, into comprehension and evaluation:

> Comprehension deals with the content of material, analysis with both content and form. One may speak of "analyzing" the *meaning* of a communication, but this usually refers to a more complex level of ability than "understanding" or "comprehending" the meaning—and that is the intention of the use of "analysis" here. It is also true that analysis shades into evaluation. . . . As one analyzes the relationships of elements of an argument, he may be judging how well the argument hangs together. (Bloom et al. 1956, pp. 144–145)

In other words, it's a mistake to suppose that a student is thinking at the level of "comprehension" whenever a teacher asks a question about the meaning of a passage. The student's behavior may be more consistent with analysis. It's also a mistake to suppose that a student is thinking at the level of "evaluation" whenever a teacher asks a student to make a judgment; that too may be analysis. Suggesting the word *meaning* as a kind of incantation to induce "comprehension," or the word *judge* to induce "evaluation" (both of which are implied in the two Web sites quoted above), misses the point. An assignment or test item is called "analysis" because of what a student does when confronted with it, not because of how it is phrased.

The confusion that occurs when teachers focus on phrasing can be revealed by a closer look at some of the question-starters. Here, for example, are six question-starters, each supposedly representing a different level of the Bloom *Taxonomy*:

> Knowledge: How did _____ happen?
> Comprehension: How would you summarize _____?
> Application: Can you make use of the facts to _____ ?
> Analysis: Why do you think _____ ?
> Synthesis: What facts can you compile _____ ?
> Evaluation: Based on what you know, how would you explain _____ ? (Fowler, 1996)

From those starters I can create these six questions:

How did World War I happen?
How would you summarize the causes of World War I?
Can you make use of the facts to explain the causes of World War I?
Why do you think World War I began?
What facts can you compile to explain the causes of World War I?
Based on what you know, how would you explain the causes of World
    War I?

Are these six different questions, each provoking a different level of student thinking? Or is there really only one question in six different formulations?

The point of this example is that levels of thinking cannot be matched up with verbal formulations. What makes a particular question an analysis-level question is that a student responds to it by analyzing. A student may correctly answer the question by luck, by copying from someone else's paper, or by recalling something said in class or read in a textbook, but none of these is what Bloom meant by "analysis."

Unfortunately, seen in this light, Bloom's *Taxonomy* isn't particularly helpful to teachers. The only way that a teacher can hope to encourage higher-order thinking (something other than recall) on an examination is to present students with material they have not already dealt with. Any question becomes (potentially) a knowledge-level question if the issue has been discussed in class. But given their need to demonstrate accountability (good test scores), teachers are understandably unwilling to ask students to answer, on a test, questions that have not already been answered in class.

If, however, one focuses on how questions are phrased rather than on what students do in response to the questions, Bloom's *Taxonomy* can be easily translated into classroom activities. This helps to explain why there are so many Web sites transforming Bloom's *Taxonomy* into lists of "key words" and question-starters. The word lists and question-starters operationalize the *Taxonomy*, and these readily available tools for classroom planning help to explain why teachers are vague about the categories even though the *Taxonomy* pervades schooling. Relying on popularizations of the *Taxonomy* that turn what was intended to be a classification of behaviors into a classification of verbal formulas, teachers are left with little of the original conception. What remains is nevertheless compelling enough to win the allegiance of vast numbers of teachers, and what remains is simply this: Recalling information is not the same as thinking with it or about it. Because of the ways that popularizations explain the *Taxonomy*, the classifications of higher mental processes may be dimly perceived, but the difference between a higher mental process and remembering a fact is clear. This immediate recognition of difference is, I believe, what accounts for the phenomenal growth of the influence of Bloom's *Taxonomy*. Thinking (we all know because we have experienced it) is a step beyond the given. It has within it an element of discovery. It is, Dewey says, "always an invasion of the unknown, a leap from the known. . . . [A] thought (what a thing suggests but is not as it presented) is creative—an incursion into the novel" (1916/1966, p. 158). And this may be what Bartlett had in mind when he identified the essence of thinking as "the use of information about something present, to get somewhere else."

But if thinking is always "a leap from the known," if it necessarily involves an unpredictable (because unknown) element, no programmatic scheme can be invented to coerce or guarantee thought. A taxonomy can be invented to classify instances of thinking after they have occurred, but it cannot show us how to create those instances. To suppose otherwise—to identify categories or levels of thinking with the use of certain words—is to encourage nonthinking. The intrusion of the prescribed formula signifies an attempt to force predictability upon the outcome of thinking. It shows the desire of teachers to manufacture discovery according to a plan, a desire that is understandable because it merges the ideal of teaching with the real-life demands of schooling, but a desire that remains, like the nature of thinking, out of reach.

DOMAINS OF THINKING

One of the perennial debates in the field of "thinking" centers on whether or not generic thinking skills exist (see, for example, McPeck, 1990). Bloom's *Taxonomy* rests on a tacit assumption that they do; that is, the categories are not limited by nor correspondent to subject matter, and examples of educational objectives and test items are drawn from across fields of study for each category in the *Taxonomy*. Even when Bloom et al. note that "no examples are given from the humanities field" to illustrate educational objectives consistent with "Application," they also say that "objectives in the application area sound very much alike, regardless of the subject matter" (1956, p. 124). Bloom's *Taxonomy* is concerned with characteristic activities or processes of thinking, and these activities or processes are assumed to be much the same regardless of what the thinker is thinking about.

There are, of course, those who reject this assumption and seek instead to clarify the concept of thinking by analyzing it, not according to levels or processes, but according to the domain or subject matter the thinking deals with, or according to the kinds of problems the thinking seeks to solve. In schools today the most familiar example of such a classification scheme is probably Howard Gardner's multiple intelligences. Gardner himself denies that in his theory he is talking about "domains" (for reasons I will go into below), but others discuss his work in precisely this way. Robert Sternberg, for example, contrasts his "theory of successful intelligence" (a combination of analytical, creative, and practical thinking) with Gardner's multiple intelligences, saying that Gardner's

> theory is not incompatible with the theory of successful intelligence, but, rather, conceptualizes intelligence(s) in a complementary way—in terms of domains rather than processes. Analytical, creative, and practical processing apply in each of Gardner's eight domains. (Sternberg, 2003, p. 7)

Obviously, Sternberg believes that, while he is attempting to clarify thinking by sketching the generic processes applied across domains, Gardner is engaged in a somewhat different project, and it is this different project that I want to examine more closely.

Gardner has argued, beginning in 1983 with *Frames of Mind*, that human intelligence is not a singular trait, but rather a family of "relatively autonomous faculties" (1999a, p. 113). Initially he identified these faculties as *linguistic, logical-mathematical, spatial, musical, bodily-kinesthetic, interpersonal*, and *intrapersonal*, but in 1999 he added *naturalist* to the list and considered *existential* as a possible ninth intelligence, though he left open whether or not it should be included. The key feature of these faculties, or intelligences, is that each designates "the ability to solve problems or to fashion products that are valued in at least one culture or community" (1999a, p. 113). Each possesses "identifiable core operations" that differentiate one intelligence from the others. The "recognition of tones and melodies," for example, is "the core of musical intelligence" just as "recognition of species membership is the core of the naturalist's intelligence" (p. 115).

While some would argue that "recognizing" or "classifying" are generic thinking skills, Gardner is saying that they are meaningful operations only when applied to a problem or product with social significance or worth. For Gardner, it is not the application of some sort of generic thinking skill (recognizing, for instance) that distinguishes instances of human thinking. Exercising one's musical intelligence differs from exercising one's naturalist intelligence because of the differences in the kinds of problems one solves and the kinds of products one fashions.

It's important at this point for me to acknowledge that Gardner identifies "eight criteria for an intelligence." (1999a, p. 113). There is more that separates the intelligences than the differences between their core operations. Here are the criteria as laid out in *Frames of Mind*:

1. Identifiable core operation(s)
2. Evolutionary history and evolutionary plausibility

3. Recognizable end-state and distinctive developmental trajectory
4. Existence of savants, prodigies, and other individuals distinguished by the presence or absence of specific abilities
5. Potential isolation by brain damage
6. Support from experimental psychological tasks
7. Support from psychometric findings
8. Susceptibility to encoding in a symbol system (pp. 113–114)

As several of these items indicate (at least items 2, 3, and 5), Gardner is attempting to link the activities of human intelligence with the structure of the brain. Whether or not this attempt succeeds (Perry Klein [2003] argues that it does not), it is important to be clear about the kind of claim Gardner is making. When he says "intelligence," Gardner is not talking about a *domain* ("an organized set of activities within a culture" [Gardner, 1999b, p. 82]). He is not talking about (for example) "physics, cooking, chess, constitutional law, and rap music." Performance within domains usually calls upon several intelligences, and a single intelligence will appear in any number of domains:

> The domain of musical performance, for example, involves bodily-kinesthetic, personal, and musical intelligences. By the same token, a particular intelligence, like spatial intelligence, can be applied in a myriad of domains, from sculpture to sailing to surgery (p. 83).

But if playing a Chopin waltz, solving a physics problem, and cooking spaghetti are not examples of "core operations," what are? What does Gardner mean by "intelligence"? The key seems to be that when Gardner says that an intelligence is "an ability to solve problems or to fashion products," he wants us to focus on the "ability" and not on either the solving/fashioning or the problems/products. An "intelligence," he says,

> refers to a biopsychological potential of our species to process certain kinds of information in certain kinds of ways. As such it clearly involves processes that are carried out by dedicated neural networks. No doubt each of the intelligences has its characteristic neural processes. (p. 94)

While it's possible to "describe certain products—for example, maps, drawings, and architectural plans—as involving a particular intelligence," the inference that these products are the work of spatial intelligence is, for Gardner, a claim about the activation of particular "neural circuitry" (p. 95). Human brains, he is saying, have developed (for evolutionary reasons) capacities to perform in ways that enable social life and culture—institutions, technologies, processes, and products.

It seems to me that Gardner is conflating the mental and the neuronal (as Ricoeur [Changeux & Ricoeur, 2000] describes these terms). On the one hand, Gardner says that an intelligence is a "core operation" such as recognition of tones and melodies. On the other hand, he says that an intelligence is the processing activity of specific neural circuitry. But neural circuits do not recognize tones. The word *recognize* points toward the anomaly. To recognize is to know again, and knowing—cognition—requires the whole brain along with the body of which it is a part and the environment in which the body-as-human-being lives and experiences. When I recognize a melody heard on the radio, what I know about the music, where I've heard it before, how it makes me feel—all this is part of the recognition. Human beings recognize tones, but neural circuits do not. To speak of recognizing a tone is to speak of human experience—the mental or the phenomenological.

There is, then, I believe, a contradiction in Gardner's two definitions of an *intelligence*, but what Gardner is trying to accomplish is a familiar goal. He wants to show how the experienced functions of human doing and creating (singing a song, cooking a meal, balancing a checkbook) can be understood as the synthesis of specific, definable neural processes. These instances of doing and creating are not themselves core operations, but rather are integrations of numerous core operations. Singing a song involves recognizing tones, but it also involves making a sound, identifying a rhythm, and many other operations, each of which individually corresponds (says Gardner) to a particular one of Gardner's intelligences. In other words, the multiple intelligences are not categories of thinking; they are categories of neural processes that contribute to thinking during the activities of solving problems and fashioning products. Thinking, Gardner is saying, appears in numerous forms, but all these forms are constructed of the eight or nine basic building blocks—the intelligences.

This reading of Gardner does not resolve the critique that he conflates the mental and the neuronal, and the question remains how a discussion of doing and creating—the experience of thinking—can come together with a discussion of "neural circuitry" in the objectified brain—that which provides what Ricoeur calls the "substrate" of thinking. How can an intelligence be a *capacity* in the sense of "one who feels the availability and limits of these powers—*I* can take, *I* can touch, and so on"—and at the same time be a *capacity* "in the vocabulary of the neurosciences" where "an entirely functional meaning. . . . does not assume that anyone feels this capacity" (Ricoeur speaking in Changeux & Ricoeur 2000, p. 84)?

I want to set aside this unanswered question and likely contradiction, however. The key point for my exploration into the causes of non-thinking is that in Gardner's theory of multiple intelligences, he asserts that the way to understand the nature of thinking is to study the eight or nine categories of neural activity. It is through combinations of these processes that all human intelligence is expressed. *Thinking* is the name we give to these combinations of neural activities.

Now, as was true with my reading of Bloom's version of Bloom's *Taxonomy*, this version of multiple intelligences is not of much use to teachers. Teachers deal with human beings, not neural circuitry. Teachers plan, implement, and assess educational experiences, not core operations (as Gardner describes them). Teachers are concerned with domains and disciplines, but intelligences "should not," says Gardner, "be confused with domains or disciplines" (1999b, p. 82). Gardner's theory seeks to isolate (analytically, at least) the individual intelligences, but because successful activity within any domain always requires "the use of several intelligences," a teacher's work never involves an intelligence in isolation (p. 83).

Despite the poor fit between the conditions of teaching and the insight offered by the theory of multiple intelligences, the theory has been enthusiastically received in schools. In an online search I did in October 2003, the search terms "Gardner multiple intelligences" yielded about 43,800 sites. Most of the first sites listed (those that receive the most hits) talked about uses of the multiple intelligences theory in schools.

What is it that makes this theory so attractive to teachers? To answer this question I am going to look at two of these Internet sites (randomly selected from those listed in the top ten of my search) to see how they portray Gardner's multiple intelligences theory.

Here is the beginning of one overview of multiple intelligences:

> Thus far Gardner has identified nine intelligences. He speculates that there may be many more yet to be identified. Time will tell. These are the paths to children's learning teachers can address in their classrooms right now. They are:
>
> > VISUAL/SPATIAL—children who learn best visually and organizing things spatially. They like to see what you are talking about in order to understand. They enjoy charts, graphs, maps, tables, illustrations, art, puzzles, costumes—anything eye catching. . . . (McKenzie, 1999)

Here is a portion of another overview:

> One of the most remarkable features of the theory of multiple intelligences is how it provides *eight different potential pathways* to learning. If a teacher is having difficulty reaching a student in the more traditional linguistic or logical ways of instruction, the theory of multiple intelligences suggests several other ways in which the material might be presented to facilitate effective learning. Whether you are a kindergarten teacher, a graduate school instructor, or an adult learner seeking better ways of pursuing self-study on any subject of interest, the same basic guidelines apply. . . .

For example, if you're teaching or learning about the law of supply and demand in economics, you might read about it (linguistic), study mathematical formulas that express it (logical-mathematical), examine a graphic chart that illustrates the principle (spatial), observe the law in the natural world (naturalist) or in the human world of commerce (interpersonal); examine the law in terms of your own body [e.g. when you supply your body with lots of food, the hunger demand goes down; when there's very little supply, your stomach's demand for food goes way up and you get hungry] (bodily-kinesthetic and intrapersonal); and/or write a song (or find an existing song) that demonstrates the law (perhaps Dylan's "Too Much of Nothing?"). (Armstrong, 2000)

The most striking similarity I see in these two excerpts is their authors' assertion that Gardner's intelligences are "paths" to learning. It's not clear what this means, but it sounds as if the intelligences are seen as alternative instructional strategies. If students aren't "learning about the law of supply and demand" satisfactorily via the teacher's usual methods, she can find in the intelligences others ways to go about her teaching. If reading the textbook and watching a movie didn't do it, perhaps singing a song will help, or maybe the students could act it out. These sorts of approaches are what Gardner characterizes as "superficial applications of the theory." While "most topics can be approached in varied ways," says Gardner, "applying a scattershot approach to each topic is a waste of time and effort" (1999b, pp. 89–90).

The notion that the intelligences are paths to learning seems to me to be a fundamental misreading of what Gardner is arguing, and it encourages the belief that "going through certain motions activates or exercises specific intelligences" (p. 90). This is an inference Gardner takes pains to repudiate. Moving one's arms or running around, he says, doesn't enhance bodily-kinesthetic intelligence "any more than babbling enhances linguistic or musical intelligence" (p. 90).

There are, in the Internet excerpts I quoted, other assertions that Gardner has specifically rejected. When the first excerpt talks about what children "like to see" and what they "enjoy," Gardner may be cringing, for he's tried to make clear "the importance of the distinction between individuals' *preferences* for materials/intelligences and their *capacities* in these spheres" (1999b, p. 81). His theory has nothing to say about what people like; it's concerned with what they are capable of. When a teacher pays close attention to which activities which students enjoy, she is probably doing something worthwhile, but she isn't talking about multiple intelligences.

Gardner is probably equally uncomfortable with talk about "children who learn best visually and organizing things spatially." This sort of language suggests confusion between "learning styles" and multiple intelligences, reminiscent of a program Gardner writes about—and condemns:

> While parts of the program were reasonable and based on research, much of it was simply a mishmash of practices, with neither scientific foundation nor clinical warrant. Left-brain and right-brain contrasts, sensory-based learning styles, "neurolinguistic programming," and MI approaches were commingled with dazzling promiscuity. (1999b, p. 79)

Over the past 10 years a number of my students have exhibited exactly this kind of intellectual promiscuity. For many of them, too, multiple intelligences, learning styles and right-brain/left-brain distinctions all amount to the same thing. Quite a few of my students over these years have chosen to speak to the rest of the class about Gardner's multiple intelligences, and the one activity most often included in these presentations has been a multiple intelligences assessment—an assessment that (as I discovered while writing this chapter) turns out to have come from the first Web site quoted above. I suspect that students other than mine—other preservice and experienced teachers—likewise derive their understanding of multiple intelligences from Web sites like these two.

The popularity of the assessment provides insight, I believe, into both what my students (and presumably other teachers as well) think multiple intelligences theory is talking about and why they find the theory so appealing. The assessment consists of statements. Here are examples:

> I enjoy categorizing things by common traits
> I believe preserving our National Parks is important
> I focus in on noise and sounds
> Remembering song lyrics is easy for me
> I get easily frustrated with disorganized people
> Religion is important to me
> Study groups are very productive for me (McKenzie, 1999)

As the examples suggest, most of the assessment is concerned with preferences—likes and dislikes—an approach that Gardner would say misses the point. Even when the assessment turns to a trait closer to a capacity (study groups are productive), it is still unlikely to elicit significant data, because of the "risks of relying on purely verbal measures of ability" (Gardner, 1999b, p. 81). If paper-and-pencil assessments of this sort provided reliable information about students, there would be no need for a theory of multiple intelligences.

Nevertheless, this sort of "assessment" of multiple intelligences is likely to remain popular for the same reason that descriptions of character derived from signs of the zodiac are popular. We enjoy reading accounts of our supposed traits, especially if some basis for the account can be supplied. Gardner's theory of multiple intelligences provides the imprimatur of science for an account of an individual's talents and uniqueness. And it provides the same scientific backing for a teacher who believes that the school day should be something more than reading, writing, and computing, something more than preparing for the next competency test. Caught between the demands for systematic, uniform instruction that will raise test scores and their own realization that no student is precisely like another, teachers are understandably attracted to a theory that champions "individually configured education" and offers a scientific rationale for it (Gardner, 1999b).

There is, however, an irony in the way the theory of multiple intelligences is employed in schooling. Teachers who are dissatisfied with the narrowness of traditional curriculum and its focus on reading, writing, and arithmetic (subjects that match up well with the first two of Gardner's intelligences—linguistic and logical-mathematical) embrace multiple intelligences and find in it a new curriculum, one for all the children. But the underlying assumption of the new curriculum is the same as that for the old curriculum: Different and predictable kinds of thinking are engendered by different activities:

> Musicians, historians, taxonomic biologists, choreographers, computer programmers, and literary critics all value critical thinking. But the *kind* of thinking required to analyze a fugue is fundamentally of a different order from that involved in observing and categorizing different species, editing a poem, debugging a computer program, or creating and revising a new dance. (p. 107)

If editing a poem and debugging a computer require different kinds of thinking (the assumption goes), then engaging in these activities means that one is thinking. A variety of assignments will (the teacher assumes) result in various kinds of thinking. All that is supposed to be necessary for successful teaching that excites students to think is to match up the kinesthetic students with the kinesthetic assignments and the intrapersonal students with the intrapersonal assignments, and so on.

Popularizations (and teachers' interpretations) of the theory of multiple intelligences may confuse "intelligences" and "domains," may mistake "preferences" for "capabilities," may jumble "intelligences" with "sensory-based learning styles" and "right-brain/left-brain" distinctions, but when it comes to the implications of the theory for education, everyone (Web site authors, teachers, and Gardner) seems to agree. Different students "have different kinds of minds," says Gardner (1999b, p. 150). Teachers who are sensitive to this truth recognize the importance of "learning about each student's backgrounds, strengths, interests, preferences, anxieties, experiences, and goals" (p. 151). This commonsense insight has, of course, long been part of teaching. But when it gets wedded to the theory of multiple intelligences, the result is not so much a deepening of insight into teaching as it is an institu-tionalization of a new set of procedures. First, discuss the reading; then view a movie, sing a song, act it out, write a journal entry about it, and so on. The teacher moves through the eight intelligences, confident that when she is done, all the students will have had their intelligence tapped and will have thought about and learned the material. Thinking, which is never routine, is assumed to be coercible by the teacher who uses the right routine.

THE PERFECTION OF THINKING

We live in our thoughts. Nothing is more familiar to human beings than thinking. But when we try to pin down what thinking is, we find ourselves using language that is as elusive as the term *thinking* itself. In schools we try to tame thinking by defining its levels or processes or by defining a variety of domains that match up with its various faces. But our pursuit of thinking bumps up against the demands and challenges of the institution of schooling and leads to the establishment of procedures that are intended to codify spon-taneity, and inevitably end up encouraging non-thinking. We try to invoke thinking by using the right words in appropriately phrased questions. We try to engage thinking by involving students in activities that utilize all of their intelligences. We behave as if discovery can be ordered up to fit the school schedule and calendar. We believe in what we are doing. But it's not clear that we are engaged in what Dewey called the "best" sense of *think-ing*—when the basis for the belief is adequate.

Are there better ways of defining *thinking* or *critical thinking* than the ones I've offered in this chapter? Are there better analyses of levels of thinking than Bloom's *Taxonomy*, better classifications of the domains of thinking than Gardner's multiple intelligences? Perhaps. But I don't believe that the encour-agements toward non-thinking that I have described can be seen as a short-coming of the definitions or of the categories created by Bloom and Gardner. The problem is that the only way to get better at defining thinking, or at ana-lyzing its levels or processes, or at classifying the domains in which different kinds of thinking operate, is to turn thinking into a predictable procedure or set of procedures. Unfortunately, this supposedly better grasp of *thinking* pro-vides students with a template to follow and alleviates the need to think. The nature of the classroom encourages such transformations because teachers need to design and employ curricula that yield desirable outcomes. They need a plan, and they may understandably feel that this leaves no room for the ungraspable.

Our pursuit of thinking bumps up against the ineffable, and our efforts to put a name to it lead to the invention of curricula that we hope are so perfectly devised that further thinking will not be necessary.

CHAPTER 2

Arts and Disciplines

Why do young people seek a college education?

This is a different question from, Why do they go to college? The answers to that second question include getting away from home, expanding their social life, and having a good time. The desire for a college education is a different matter, as evidenced by the responses I've got when I've put this question to groups of high-school seniors on college-visiting days. Not surprisingly, they are, at first, silent. In part this is because they don't expect to be questioned, but even more so because the question is so eccentric. Everyone wants a college education. Eventually, when they discover that I won't answer the question for them and that I really do expect an answer, they respond: "I want to get a good job."

They don't always use exactly those words. Sometimes they talk about "getting ahead" or "being successful," but the expectations of the high-school seniors (and parents) I've encountered are clear: College will prepare them for a profession. This is not a surprising expectation, but it is somewhat ironic, considering the purpose of the sessions in which I've posed this question. I meet the students and their parents as a spokesperson for the university's general education program, and I am supposed to enlighten them about the 50 hours of coursework (out of 124 required for graduation) that they must complete, but that won't count toward a major—that don't, in other words, seem to have much to do with their profession.

The burden of a college education (for career preparation) that happens to include weighty general-education requirements that apparently have nothing to do with a career tends to be one of those curious facts of life that people reluctantly accept as a necessary and inexplicable evil. But our willingness to accept that this is what school is like prevents us from asking some important questions: Is the learning in a general-education course somehow a different kind of learning from that in a course preparing us for a career?

Is the thinking that we do in the one different in kind or degree or purpose from the thinking that we do in the other? How is one subject different from another? And, finally, the question that students do often ask (though typically it's not taken seriously): Why do I have to learn this? That is, Why should I study American history or geometry or philosophy? Why should I complete a sequence of general education courses at all?

These are not new questions, of course. At the beginning of Plato's dialogue *Protagoras*, Socrates relates a discussion with a young man named Hippocrates, who is so enthusiastic to become a student of the sophist Protagoras that he says, "I'd bankrupt myself and my friends too," if that's all it would take to be accepted as a student. Protagoras, explains the boy, has "a monopoly on wisdom" (310e; all quotes from Plato, 1997). But before the two go inside to see the famed sophist, Socrates argues for caution. If Hippocrates were to study with a physician, he would learn what he needed in order to become (like his namesake) a physician. If he were to study with a sculptor, he would learn what he needed in order to become a sculptor.

"And," continues Socrates, "if somebody asks you what you expect to become in going to Protagoras?"

Hippocrates blushes, admitting that it seems he would "become a sophist" (312a).

At this point, however, Socrates considers an alternative way of looking at the matter. "Maybe," he says,

> this isn't the sort of education you expect to get from Protagoras. Maybe you expect to get the kind of lessons you got from your grammar instructor or music teacher or wrestling coach. You didn't get from them technical instruction to become a professional, but a general education suitable for a gentleman. (312b)

The contrast Socrates draws in these lines reflects that same issue of career preparation versus general education. There are, he is saying, two kinds of education. One is a technical education that leads to the practice of an art (or occupation). The other is a liberal education that leads to a way of life. Professional education (the studies that lead to becoming a doctor or a musician) differs (in some presumably significant ways) from general education (the studies shared by all students, or at least by those destined to become gentlemen).

Because the distinction between technical and liberal is so familiar, readers of the dialogue probably do not think to ask what it is that makes the difference. How is the education one gets from the sculptor different from that which one gets from the music teacher? Presumably the differences lie in the subjects themselves, but what makes the subject "sculpting" so different from the subject "music"? Is it a question of the content or subject matter or principles of sculpting and music? Is it a question of the methods of instruction that are employed? Is it a question of the purposes that are proposed for instruction?

In this chapter I'm going to attempt to answer these questions and, along the way, to argue that our current notions of fields of study, subject matter, disciplines, content, lessons—the stuff that teaching is supposed to be about—are confused remnants of ancient ideas and that while the language of "technical" and "liberal" is still used, much of the ancient distinction has been lost. One result of this desiccation of educational thinking has been uncertainty about how to explain or defend the assertion that everyone should study a defined group of subjects, and with this uncertainty has come the partitioning of instruction within subjects in ways that have encouraged non-thinking. To make this case, though, I need to go back 2½ millennia to take a closer look at the sort of education Socrates called "suitable for a gentleman."

BODY AND SOUL

In Plato's *Republic*, when Socrates first takes up the question of how to educate the guardians of his utopian city, he turns to what he sees as traditional Greek education:

> What will their education be? Or is it hard to find anything better than that which has developed over a long period—physical training for bodies and music and poetry for the soul? (376e; all quotes from Plato, 1997)

How should we understand these twin pillars of ancient Greek education—physical training and music? When Socrates offers the education of the body and the soul as the proper education for the guardians of his city, he is echoing, as he says, "that which has developed over a long period." This is not merely a Platonic ideal, but a way of life that already, when Socrates was alive, had a long history in the city-states of Greece and would eventually spread across much of the Mediterranean world. The Greek gymnasium and palestra (the "sports ground" where children were coached in running, jumping, and throwing) would be incorporated into the Roman bath, and the centrality of sport would remain a hallmark of the Hellenic way of life for centuries (Marrou 1964, p. 69). At the heart of this way of life lies education. When Pericles tells the Athenians in his famous funeral oration that they are the school of Hellas, that they have taught the Greeks how to be Greek, he is arguing that the essence of Greek identity lies not in racial inheritance, but in education—in *paideia*. The union of the healthy body and soul is what it means to be Greek. Education through physical training and music turns a child into a citizen, one who is able to take part in the life of the Greek city.

We use some of this same sort of language to describe our educational aims today. Many of the teachers I have worked with have told me that they prepare children to become useful members of society, but this surface similarity obscures deeper levels of disagreement about what constitutes a useful member of society and about what sort of teaching is required to achieve the aim. I suspect that none of the teachers I have ever known would agree with the Athenian who says in Plato's *Laws*,

> So by an "uneducated" man we shall mean a man who has not been trained to take part in a chorus; and we must say that if a man *has* been sufficiently trained, he is "educated." . . . And this means that a well-educated man will be able to sing and dance *well*. (654b; all quotes from Plato, 1997)

As unlikely as this notion of "educated" sounds to modern ears, it fits with the centrality of physical training and music in Greek life. Performance in a chorus (not a score on a test) demonstrates the accomplishments of one who has received a proper education in physical training and music. This performance should not, however, be thought of as what is today commonly called a "performance assessment." Singing and dancing are done not to show that something has been learned, but rather because they are part of living well.

I call this "living well" (or what often appears in translations of Aristotle's writings as "happiness") to highlight the intrinsic quality of the goods that this sort of education aims to engender.

> An educational process has an *intrinsic* end if its result lies entirely within the *person* being educated, an excellence or perfection of his person, an improvement built right into his nature as a good habit is part of the nature of the person in whom the power is habituated. An *extrinsic* end of education, on the other hand, lies in the goodness of an *operation*, not as reflecting the goodness of the operator but rather the perfection of something else as a result of the operation being performed well (Adler, 1951/1977, p. 95).

The aim of music lessons can be to create competence in performance (or competence in appreciation, for that matter); or the aim of the lessons can be to create a musical person. The former is an extrinsic aim, the cultivation of an operation, and is thus an example of technical or professional education. The latter is an intrinsic aim, the cultivation of a person, and is thus an example of general or liberal education. This ambiguity about what a music lesson can accomplish shows that the distinction between technical and liberal is not strictly correlated with fields of study. But if the distinction between technical and liberal is not a question of subject matter or content, on what does it depend? Are there certain kinds of lessons or teaching methods that foster intrinsic or extrinsic outcomes? To address these questions, I want to look next at a change in Greek education that was occurring already in the age of Socrates.

TRIUMPH OF THE CLASSROOM

What would the modern student of education, transported to ancient Greece, make of the children marching and singing or competing on the palestra? I suspect that these sights would be viewed as interesting extracurricular activities and that the modern educator would continue to search for Greek classrooms.

And she would find them. Just as children were instructed by a music teacher and an athletic coach, they were also given writing lessons by a grammar teacher. The modern educator would find the writing lessons to be the most recognizable form of education in ancient Greece. Children, who would begin school at about age 7, sat in a classroom in rows and copied letters, syllables, and words provided by the grammar teacher. Once these basics were mastered, the children might move on (under the tutelage of a different kind of teacher) to literature, probably Homer and Hesiod.

But it would be a mistake to think of the lessons of the grammar teacher as the center of the school day, much less career preparation. The schools of ancient Greece were not attempting to create a class of scribes. Nor were the lessons of the grammar teacher viewed as the most essential or fundamental component of education.

The relative insignificance of school studies in the educational scheme is suggested in Plato's *Protagoras*. The sophist Protagoras, seeking students who have completed their school studies, explains how his instruction differs from that offered by others:

> The others abuse young men, steering them back again, against their will, into subjects the likes of which they have escaped from at school, teaching them arithmetic, astronomy, geometry, music, and poetry . . . but if he comes to me, he will learn only what he has come for. What I teach is sound deliberation. . . . (318e–319a)

Even when the school subjects have been expanded, so that arithmetic, astronomy, and geometry have been added to the traditional music and poetry, they are still (for Protagoras) just a prelude to, or support for, a genuine education. In this he agrees with Plato and Socrates and the traditional Greek perspective. What makes the claim of Protagoras so revolutionary—

and so objectionable to Socrates—is the assertion that living well can be taught in the same way that the Greek alphabet can be taught, that the methods (and perhaps materials) of the grammar teacher can achieve the highest educational outcomes. Protagoras is claiming that he can teach young men to live well by teaching them how to think. He expands on this position later in the dialogue:

> [T]he greatest part of a man's education is to be in command of poetry, by which I mean the ability to understand the words of the poets, to know when a poem is correctly composed and when not, and to know how to analyze a poem and to respond to questions about it. (339a)

When Protagoras speaks of being "in command of poetry," he has ceased to think of poetry as a dimension of music. It is not the traditional aim of learning and reciting poetry that he has in mind, but rather something much more in keeping with our contemporary views about the study of literature. It involves the study of a specialized vocabulary (Homer's language was already archaic), the study of literary forms and devices, and the study of critical techniques. Armed with these tools, the educated young man is able to respond correctly to any poem he encounters. Where the older approach to poetry grew out of an oral tradition, this approach takes the written word as the starting point. The educated young man (according to Protagoras) is one who can analyze and judge a poem when it is presented to him.

The clash between the traditional approach to poetry and that of Protagoras plays out in his dialogue with Socrates, but whoever gets the better of the argument between Socrates and Protagoras, it is Protagoras who foreshadows the direction that formal education will take. Protagoras—both in his life and in the dialogue that bears his name—is arguing (against Socrates and Plato) that virtue, or living well, can be directly taught, that it does not depend on the indirect influence or habituation of traditional physical training and music. In time, schools in the Hellenic world and the Roman Empire would come to embrace both his rhetorical treatment of literature and his belief that the highest ends of education could be reached through the sort of direct instruction that had once been the province of the lowly grammar-teacher (with the esteem of this method of instruction elevated no doubt by its employment in the hands of the *rhetor*—the teacher of rhetoric). Protagoras was among those transforming the way that "liberal arts" were studied by merging the methods of technical education with the ends of general education. He is saying that there is no distinction of method between professional and liberal studies.

But if neither subject matter nor method of instruction adequately accounts for the distinction between professional and liberal education (or technical and general education), what remains? To say that the difference lies only in the outcome (is the outcome, in the language of Adler, development of a person or development of an operation?) really means that there is no instructional difference, no difference that can be defined in terms of the content to be treated or the ways in which teachers treat that content. All subject matter is (potentially) liberal and professional, technical and general. Before embracing this conclusion, however, I want to consider another way to think about what it is we are trying to differentiate when we use a term like *liberal education*. What is the place of knowledge and knowing in liberal and professional studies? To pursue this question, I want to turn to the subject that Plato offered as the one best suited for turning the soul toward "what is."

MATHEMATICS AND KNOWING

From the modern point of view, the Greek tradition of a general education that consists of physical training and music leaves out more than a few essentials. For one thing, it seems too exclusively concerned with the humanities. In the United States today the states divide about evenly between those that require 3 years of mathematics and science in high school and those that require 2 years of each. Four states require 4 years of mathematics, and many others require 4 years of mathematics and science if a student is to receive an "honors" or similar diploma. And all this of course is on top of the mathematics and science taught in elementary and middle school.

Mathematics and the sciences were not, however, absent from the Greek curriculum. Plato, writing at a time when mathematical studies were flourishing, was one of those urging greater attention to mathematics. In fact, Plato seems to have seen mathematical studies as the lynchpin of education. In book 7 of the *Republic*, Socrates asks what subject it is "that draws the soul from the realm of becoming to the realm of what is." Having decided that it cannot be physical training or music that achieves this end, Socrates turns to "the crafts." These (building and making) too are rejected as subjects that turn the soul to "what is" because "the crafts all seem to be base and mechanical" (522b). Glaucon (Socrates' interlocutor) accepts this conclusion, but it stumps him. "Apart from music and poetry, physical training, and the crafts," he wonders, "what subject is left?" In other words, this brief list—music and poetry, physical training, and the crafts—sums up all the curricular categories Glaucon can imagine, and Socrates agrees. "Well, if we can't find anything apart from these," he says, "let's consider one of the subjects that touches all of them" (522b). What he is looking for is that common thing that every craft, every type of thought, and every science uses and that is among the first compulsory subjects for everyone.... That inconsequential matter of distinguishing the one, the two, and the three. In short, I mean number and calculation, for isn't it true that every craft and science must have a share in that? (522c)

Socrates goes on to argue that "calculation and arithmetic"—the sort of things taught to young children in their earliest schooling—possess a peculiar ability to turn the soul toward "what is." The issue for him seems to be that when we recognize something as a unity, we "see the same thing to be both one and an unlimited number at the same time" (525a). It is the ambiguity that Socrates sees as essential, because the soul, to begin its journey toward what is, must first be puzzled (524a). Knowledge, as Socrates understands it, begins with puzzlement. Puzzling or perplexing the person he is questioning—or "numbing" him, as Meno complains in the dialogue of the same name—is one of the common features of Socratic encounters (80a–b; all quotes from Plato, 1997). Because numbers have the power to stir the understanding and "calculation and arithmetic are wholly concerned with numbers," it follows that calculation and arithmetic "lead us toward truth" (524e, 525a, 525b).

At least, Socrates adds, the "subject of calculation" turns the soul toward truth "provided that one practices it for the sake of knowing rather than trading" (525d). This important proviso provides deep insight into the Platonic conception of knowing and knowledge. Admittedly, Socrates dismisses the use of arithmetic for "buying and selling" in part because the activities of "tradesmen and retailers" are beneath the dignity of warriors and philosophers, but there is another, deeper reason. Those who use arithmetic for the sake of trading make the mistake of always attaching numbers "to visible or tangible bodies," and this prevents them from discussing "the numbers themselves" (526d). However competent they are as arithmeticians, tradesmen (from Socrates and Plato's point of view) are still trapped in the cave, still living in the world of shadows. They are capable when buying and selling, but they don't know anything about numbers.

This proviso about how the "subject of calculation" should be used obviously bears on the distinction between professional and liberal studies. Calculation can be a liberal study, but only if it is detached from business. Again, the end or purpose of instruction is taken as the key for determining whether a subject is liberal or professional: Are its aims intrinsic (the development of the person) or extrinsic (the development of an operation)?

But Socrates is not saying that tradesmen cannot study calculation in a liberal manner, that someone who intends to earn a living by selling olive oil cannot—because of that intention—seek truth through the study of numbers. More important than the professional ambitions of the student is the manner in which numbers are studied. While Socrates does not elaborate in the *Republic* how the study of numbers should be conducted, he does demonstrate what he has in mind in the dialogue *Meno*. Socrates questions a slave about a geometry problem: From a given square (with a side of 2 feet), a line of what length is needed to construct a square twice as big?

In his demonstration Socrates first allows the slave to make a guess, and the slave answers confidently that the new line will be twice as long as one of the sides of the original square, or a length of 4 feet. Further questions lead the slave to see that this answer is wrong, and he makes a second guess—3 feet. When questioning leads the slave to see that this answer is also wrong, the slave confesses his complete confusion (an attitude that Socrates praises as necessary for any learning to commence). A new line of questions leads the slave to announce that he now sees that a square based on the diagonal of the original square (Socrates gives him the word *diagonal*) will be twice the size of the original.

For the purposes of understanding the Platonic notion of liberal education, a key element of this demonstration is that the slave *sees* how things are for himself. The lesson is not about the wrongness and rightness of his answers; it's about seeing in the world and seeing with the mind's eye. This, it seems to me, is crucial for understanding how geometry, calculation, or any other mathematical study can be pursued in what Plato believes is a liberal manner. Socrates could easily have asked the slave the geometry question and then have explained that the Pythagorean theorem can be applied to answer the question. That is, he could have begun by teaching the slave the language of the Pythagorean theorem, or presenting the slave with this piece of knowledge—except that it is Socrates' (and Plato's) position that knowing is a matter of seeing the intelligible, seeing beyond the shadows. To create a "lesson" that turns the soul toward "what is" requires resisting the impulse to begin with the finished piece of knowledge. Quoting the Pythagorean theorem, or even using it to answer a question, is the sort of use that tradesmen make of numbers: It doesn't require thinking or knowing anything.

This stance clearly puts Socrates at odds with our current U.S. educational practice of prescribing (at the state or district level) guidelines for instruction in arithmetic (and every other subject). Examples could be drawn from the curriculum guides of almost any state. Standard 7.4.3 in Indiana's Academic Standards (a mathematics standard for seventh graders) begins: "Know and understand the Pythagorean Theorem." Standards for subsequent grade levels return to and build upon this knowledge. What these standards mean by "know" is something quite different from what Socrates means. In one case, knowing begins with certainty; in the other it begins with perplexity. In one case, knowing is demonstrated by recapitulation of the known. In the other, knowing is experienced rather than demonstrated. In one case, the hard work of thinking has already been done on the material that the teacher presents to the student. In the other, the teacher inquires in conjunction with the student's thinking. These differences in ways (or concepts) of knowing make up a significant part of the difference between a liberal and a professional study as Plato and Socrates understand the difference, but the Platonic conception of knowing is not to be found in current U.S. curricular policy, and in fact, it was already being displaced during Plato's life. To show why, I'm going to pick up the historical thread and follow the story of how the medieval seven liberal arts (the primary source of our modern ideas about general education) grew out of the Greek *paideia*.

THE SEVEN LIBERAL ARTS

When Socrates makes his case for mathematics in book 7 of the *Republic*, he doesn't stop with "arithmetic and calculation." The second mathematical study he recommends is geometry, again with a caveat like that attached to the study of calculation. "Therefore, if geometry compels the soul to study being, it's appropriate, but if it compels it to study becoming, it's inappropriate" (526e). Socrates then complains that "practical men," when they talk about geometry, give "ridiculous accounts" because they are always talking about "doing things. They talk of 'squaring,' 'applying,' 'adding,' and the like, whereas the entire subject is pursued for the sake of knowledge" (527a).

The problem that Socrates has with "practical men" seems to be that they want to use geometry to answer questions and solve problems. Like Glaucon, they think of geometry "as it pertains to war" and talk about how geometry helps when "setting up a camp, occupying a region, concentrating troops, deploying them," or in general managing an army "in battle or on the march" (526d). Socrates grants the possibility of these applications but sees them as trivial. "A little geometry—or calculation for that matter"—is enough to deal with such matters. "What we need to consider," says Socrates, "is whether the greater and more advanced part of [geometry] tends to make it easier to see the form of the good" (526d).

We might see his question in these terms: Teaching children about shape and measurement has obvious practical applications, from putting up wallpaper to mowing lawns, but these practical applications don't require working with theorems, axioms, and proofs. So how do we justify compelling students to study the "more advanced part" of geometry? Socrates' answer is that "we must require those in your fine city not to neglect geometry" because "it draws the soul toward truth and produces philosophic thought"

(527b–c). Geometry—if it is pursued as a liberal study—will lead (says Socrates) to thinking, in fact, to the only genuine kind of thought, because it is only when we turn away from tangible things (which are really just shadows) that we discover knowledge.

This Platonic answer to the question "Why study geometry?" has no place in current educational thinking, in which practical applications epitomize knowing and knowledge, but the question remains. If geometry is valuable (for almost all students) only as a technical or professional study, why pursue it beyond its professional payoff? A variety of answers to this question emerges with the development of the concept of the "liberal arts," most of them beginning with the claim that possession of the liberal arts is what it means to be educated. This claim echoes Pericles' statement that one must be educated to become a true Greek, but as Western scholars defined the "liberal arts," they also redefined what "educated" meant, and of course redefined what "thinking" meant. To spell out this redefinition, I want to finish my sketch of Plato's contribution to the concept of the liberal arts and of what happened to that contribution.

Arguing in book 7 of the *Republic* for the importance of arithmetic and plane geometry for a proper education, Socrates goes on to add solid geometry, astronomy, and harmonics to the list. The mathematical progression moves, then, from number, to shape in two dimensions, to shape in three dimensions, to the motion of solid objects (perceived by the eye), and finally to a parallel motion perceived by the ear. Socrates sees the last mathematical subject as the attempt to "seek out the numbers to be found in these audible consonances [of harmonic intervals]" (531c), making "harmonics" a quite different study from the "music" of traditional Greek education. The full list of mathematical subjects—arithmetic and calculation, plane geometry, solid geometry, astronomy, and harmonics—is not, of course, a curriculum that was followed in any school, but it influenced later thinkers about what ought to be included in a complete education.

Much of the educational tradition of the Greek *enkuklios paideia* ("circle of education" or "ordinary education") was adopted by the Romans. In the first century B.C.E. Marcus Terrentius Varro described nine liberal arts in his *Nine Books of Disciplines (Disciplinarum Libri IX)*. What had been for Plato "music and poetry" was now three subjects: grammar, rhetoric, and dialectic. Plato's mathematical subjects were included (with plane and solid geometry being combined into a single subject). Architecture and medicine were added to complete the list of nine disciplines. Varro's work was lost during the early Middle Ages, but it had considerable influence on Western education, serving as a primary source for Martianus Capella.

Early in the 5th century of the modern era, Martianus completed his *Marriage of Philology and Mercury (De Nuptiis Philologiae et Mercurii)*.

This remarkably popular textbook offered "a well-proportioned and comprehensive account of all the liberal arts in the compass of one comfortable-sized book" (Stahl, 1971, p. 22). The book opens with Mercury's search for a wife. Apollo "advises him to marry Philology, an astonishingly erudite young lady" (Stahl, 1971, p. 24). At the wedding, Mercury presents a dowry of seven handmaids to his wife. They are "seven sisters, personifications of the seven disciplines," and they represent in allegorical form the union of eloquence and learning, rhetoric and philosophy, thus bringing together the aims of Protagoras and Socrates (Stahl, 1971, p. 24). The first three sisters stand for what will come to be known as the "trivium"—grammar, rhetoric, and dialectic. These are the subjects Protagoras professed to master and offered to teach young men in order to develop in them "sound deliberation." The last four sisters stand for what will come to be known as the "quadrivium"—arithmetic, geometry, astronomy, and music. These are the subjects Socrates offered as a way of turning the soul to "what is," a way of discovering knowledge.

Until the time of Martianus the composition of the liberal arts had not been fixed. Some attempts (such as Varro's nine disciplines) had been made, but there had been no agreement about the number or sequence of the arts. Vitruvius had listed "literature, drawing, geometry, optics, arithmetic, history, philosophy, music, medicine, law, and astronomy"; Seneca had limited his list to "literature, music, geometry, arithmetic, and astronomy"; and Galen had added "sculpture and drawing" as optional subjects to a basic list of "medicine, rhetoric, music, geometry, arithmetic, dialectics, astronomy, literature, and law" (Gwynn, 1926, p. 85). Within two generations of Martianus, however, the canon of seven liberal arts was established as both Boethius and Cassiodorus wrote influential works about the seven liberal arts. Boethius has been credited with creating the two categories of trivium and quadrivium. Cassiodorus helped to firmly establish the number of liberal arts at seven by linking them with the seven "pillars of wisdom" mentioned in the Bible (Proverbs 9:1).

Perhaps the most significant feature of the 5th-century codification is the choice of the "arts" that are not included in the canon. The emphasis on sport that had given Hellenic education its special character was gone. The disappearance was not, of course, a sudden event. Seneca, writing about the "arts" in the first century C.E. followed Posidonius, who, a century earlier,

> classified the arts under four heads. First place was given to the arts that teach virtue; second place to the arts "which the Greeks call ἐγκύκλιοι and the Romans *liberales*"; third place to the "frivolous" arts of dancing, singing, painting, and sculpture; and fourth place to all the arts that involve manual labor (Gwynn, 1926, p. 88).

Schools of the Middle Ages dealt with only the second of Posidonius's four categories. The rest of the categories, which had been a part of Greek education, made their way into modern schools but remain incidental to the main business of schooling, which is (as it has been since the age of Martianus) primarily concerned with the arts that "the Greeks call ἐγκύκλιοι and the Romans *liberales*." In the United States when school budgets are reduced, it is the "'frivolous' arts" and the manual arts that are first cut, while the "arts that teach virtue" (presumably philosophy) have rarely been a significant part of public schooling.

Together, trivium and quadrivium formed a curriculum employed in schools in the West for 1,000 years. When Gregor Reisch produced the image titled *The Student's Progress* in 1504 (more than 1,000 years after the death of Martianus), he showed a (literal) tower of learning, with its first four levels composed of the seven liberal arts—trivium and quadrivium. At the top of the tower are moral and physical philosophy, with theology at the pinnacle (Rait, 1912). The picture testifies to the conception of the liberal arts that had emerged during the Middle Ages—a sequence of studies preparatory to higher learning. This notion of the liberal arts suggests an answer different from the one that Socrates gave to the question "Why study geometry?" Geometry (or any of the other six liberal arts) is studied because it helps to prepare the student for higher learning. In the first century of the Roman Empire, this meant preparation for oratory. Quintilian, the foremost teacher and rhetorician of the age asked,

> [H]ow will music benefit the orator? The answer is severely practical: It will teach him to control and modulate his voice, and make harmonious gestures. Similarly geometry is to be studied partly for the excellent mental training that it gives, partly for its practical utility when the orator has to speak of such subjects as land measurement or more intricate mathematical problems. (quoted in Gwynn, 1926, p. 197)

As the empire disintegrated and the Christian church became a more potent influence on daily life than civil authority had been, church fathers worried about the pagan origins of the liberal arts, but the arts were nevertheless adopted as an appropriate preparation for reading the Bible. After about 1200 c.e., the liberal arts began to be seen as the appropriate preparation for young men who wished to attend a university. The liberal studies had become professional studies as a new profession was born—the academic, the scholar.

As the liberal arts became codified and entrenched in Western schooling, they were part of the establishment of a fundamental educational concept, one so fundamental, so taken for granted, that recognizing it as an intellectual creation takes some imagination. The liberal arts became the template of what a "discipline" is, and as this concept of "discipline" settled in, notions of knowing and thinking inevitably followed.

THE NATURE OF A DISCIPLINE

When someone wants to know about a child's school life, one of the most common questions asked is "What are you studying?" It's a question that fits a student of any age, and it's easily answered: "I take reading and spelling and arithmetic"; "I take biology and world geography and algebra"; "I'm taking a humanities class and a physics class and a history class."

Schools have been organized—in their physical structure, personnel, divisions of the day and of the year, and materials and equipment—around the idea of studying nameable disciplines. It is our sense of what these disciplines are about and of what studying them requires that determines the activities of education, the settings in which it occurs, and the materials used to accomplish its aims. Because the concept of a "discipline" is at the heart of education, when we attempt to explain why a student needs to study, say, geometry, we are also (whether we realize it or not) attempting to explain what qualifies as a discipline. This means explaining not only what subject matter is important enough for the teacher (and therefore the students) to take notice of but also what sort of doing or thinking turns an ordinary activity of life into a discipline.

How have the liberal arts come to define the concept of a "discipline"? To answer this question I want to return to the portrayal Martianus Cappella gives of the "seven sisters" and their domains. What do these discussions of the liberal arts in *The Marriage of Philology and Mercury* consist of?

Martianus offers a compendium of learning culled from numerous sources. For example, in the book on geometry he draws on Solinus, Pliny, Varro, and Euclid (Stahl, 1971, pp. 125 ff.), and he describes Archimedes and Euclid as observers of the wedding. Curiously, his main sources were Solinus and Pliny, neither of whom is noted for his mathematical learning, but then Martianus's treatment is not primarily concerned with what we call geometry. His notion of the discipline is indicated in the way he describes the bridesmaid Geometry. She wears a gown with "figures depicting celestial orbits and spheres . . . intervals, weights, and measures," and she carries a geometer's rule and globe. The most startling aspect of her appearance is her shoes—dirty and shredded. Geometry has been traveling the earth, and Martianus reminds readers that her name means "earth-measuring" (Stahl, 1971, pp. 125–126).

In keeping with this introduction, the bulk of the book is a description of the known world. The size of the earth is given—through the estimates of both Ptolemy and Eratosthenes—and Martianus attempts to explain how Eratosthenes computed his result, but his explanation makes no sense, as Martianus apparently does not understand the mathematics. He goes on to divide the world into three continents (Europe, Asia, and Africa) and names the rivers, straits, and seas that define the continents. Then he launches into a whirlwind tour, naming regions, peoples, and geographical features. On his tour of Africa, he describes the "wonders of the dark continent," including "grotesque monsters" and the source of the Nile—"in a lake in Mauretania" (Stahl, 1971, pp. 138–139). Besides place-names and locations, he includes a few measurements—the distance from India to Cadiz, that from the Ethiopian Ocean to the Don River—and notes sources for these distances and disputes among the sources.

Having evidently heard enough of these matters, the wedding guests direct Geometry to get on with a proper discussion of her topic, and in the few remaining pages of the book, Martianus provides a survey of Euclidean geometry, consisting of classifications and definitions of figures, lines, solids, angles, and proportions. Finally he gives Euclid's five postulates, some definitions, and some material that does not come from Euclid.

In essence, the survey of geometry that Martianus provides is much like the survey of his book on geometry that I have just provided. Like him, I have given a hasty and incomplete version of the topic, and like his, my version has relied on intermediate sources rather than the original. Just as Martianus wrote knowingly about subjects he did not understand, I have alluded to Eratosthenes' calculation of the circumference of the earth without adding that I don't know that I could explain the procedure on my own, much less make the calculations myself. Have I (like Martianus) included mistakes and misunderstandings? Not intentionally, but then neither did he.

My point is that the practice of selecting, amending, condensing, and reordering information from authorized sources is an important aspect of what we mean by a discipline, even in the experimental sciences, in which experiments are shaped by what scientists have learned about the work of others. This business of digesting information is a practice that depends upon literacy, for part of the nature of a discipline is that it has a history. It is a culmination of efforts over time—perhaps generations, perhaps millennia. It is a culmination because when the information is presented, it is shown as fixed and finished. There may be debates (says Martianus) about the size of the earth, but this is what Eratosthenes says and this is what Ptolemy says, and their sayings are fixed and finished. A discipline (in the tradition of the liberal arts) is a collection of these sayings.

Those who have worked in recent years in the United States writing educational "standards" will find my definition of *discipline* to be rather obvious. What is a set of standards but a compendium of the content of a field of study derived from authoritative writing? What else could it be?

To suggest an answer to that last question, I want to return to Socrates and his discussion in book 7 of the *Republic* of the mathematical subjects that turn the soul toward "what is." Earlier I noted without comment that Socrates adds solid geometry to his list, placing it after plane geometry. The matter is not, however, quite as simple as that. What happens is that Socrates first suggests that astronomy should come after geometry; then almost immediately he decides that this is an error.

> After plane surfaces, we went on to revolving solids before dealing with solids by themselves. But the right thing to do is to take up the third dimension right after the second. And this, I suppose, consists of cubes and of whatever shares in depth (528a–b).

Glaucon agrees but raises a difficulty: "[T]his subject hasn't been developed yet" (528b). In other words, solid geometry was not yet a discipline because there were no authoritative sources one could turn to. We can't ask students to study this (says Glaucon) because we haven't anything for them to study.

Socrates, however, does not find this to be an insurmountable challenge, even though what he is advocating would be comparable to someone calling for university study of evolutionary biology in 1649—100 years before Comte de Buffon's *Histoire naturelle, géneralle et particulière* and 210 years before Darwin's *Origin of Species*. The reasons the subject of solid geometry has not been developed (Socrates says) are that "no city values it" and that there has been no "director" to guide the research: "The researchers need a director, for, without one, they won't discover anything" (528b). Socrates is confident that "if the subject was consistently and vigorously pursued, it would soon be developed" (528c).

When Socrates talks about "the subject" of the "dimension of depth," he cannot have in mind a collection of the sayings of authoritative sources. He cannot be thinking about "the subject" in terms of selecting, amending, condensing, and reordering information. But if "the subject" is not some body of information, what is it?

The answer may lie in the Greek idea of a *techne*—"a systematic and complete body of knowledge deriving from a clear beginning point (or principle)" (Wagner, 1983, p. 32). In Latin, *techne* becomes *ars*, the arts, so that the liberal arts are just one family of *technes*. Each science, Aristotle had taught, depends upon its own principles, its own "'art,' framed by human reason and binding together the details of knowledge in a single, coherent system" (Gwynn, 1926, p. 89). Perhaps Socrates is saying that while "the subject" of the "dimension of depth" is not yet a *techne* because it is in "a ridiculous state," lacking systematic and complete knowledge, there are nevertheless indications of a beginning point or principle. Perhaps he has in mind the geometry lesson with the slave and supposes that just as some of the properties of squares can be teased out through a judicious line of questioning, so too the properties of cubes and spheres may yield to inquiry. Obviously, such inquiries require a director, or, as Socrates sometimes calls himself, a midwife—someone to pose the questions that will lead to the revelation of first principles.

Applying the term *midwife* to this Socratic notion of a discipline (or at least of a school subject) reminds us of how Socrates views the student's relationship to knowledge. Socrates assumes that the student already possesses understanding of the principles that guide inquiry into the subject of geometry (remember the slave!); it's simply a matter of bringing forth this understanding. In part the process involves naming things—just as Martianus names peoples, geographical landforms, regions, mathematical relationships, harmonic proportions, and all of the other knowledge he categorizes. In the dialogue *Cratylus*, Socrates acknowledges the importance of naming: "Don't we instruct each other, that is to say, divide things according to their natures? . . . a name is a tool for giving instruction, that is to say, for dividing being" (388b–c; all quotes from Plato, 1961). But the essential effort of Socratic inquiry is not the manipulation or reproduction of names. In the geometry demonstration from *Meno*, although Socrates takes pains to insist, "I am not teaching the boy anything, but all I do is question him," he does in fact tell the slave the name of the line that connects one corner of a square with its opposite—*diagonal* (82e). The fact that the slave can use this word is largely irrelevant to the inquiry, however. What matters is that the slave recognizes how this name is an instance of "dividing being." The slave comes to see something about squares that he had not seen before. The name *diagonal* he got from Socrates, but the revelation comes from within the slave himself. At least, this is the case Socrates wants to make: No teacher can turn a student's soul toward "what is." All the teacher can do is ask the right questions. Knowledge does not, says Socrates, lie outside the student in the form of an external corpus of information called a "discipline." Knowledge lies within the student. Thinking about geometry (Socrates wants to show) is not a matter of finding out what Euclid said; it's a matter of finding out (through the strength of our own inquiry) the truth about points, lines, shapes, and solids.

THE CHILD AND THE CURRICULUM

What I have tried to show in this chapter is how contemporary notions about fields of study, subject matter, disciplines, content, and lessons—the stuff that teaching is about—have their roots in ancient educational theory and practice, especially in debates about liberal and professional studies. One of the legacies of this history has been its effect on how thinking has been understood in schools.

To begin with, education has become schooling. "For us," says Marrou (1964, p. 206), "the cardinal problem in education is the school. There was no comparable problem for the ancients." There was no comparable problem because school—the classroom lessons of a grammar teacher—was a small and relatively insignificant part of education. So complete is the identification of education with schooling today that when we say of an experience, "That was a real education!" we are always talking about an experience that occurred outside school. We use the exclamation to express the irony of a situation in which education has been separated from schooling. For the study of thinking and non-thinking, the identification of education with schooling is the most significant element in the history of the liberal arts because education in its large sense is the evidence, process, and product of thinking. As the moral and intrinsic aims of education were absorbed by the schools, thinking tended to become scholastic, bounded by the aims and procedures of the classroom. Thinking was separated from ordinary life.

Education has also become increasingly linked to literacy in its broadest sense—the use of written language and numbers. The time devoted to the lessons of the grammar teacher expanded until they became the most significant part of the school day. With this emphasis on literacy, thinking has come to be viewed as an activity dependent upon words and numbers. Thinking is seen as what we do to and with these tools.

Along with the emphasis on literacy has necessarily come a de-emphasis on physical training. The gymnastics and sports that were the most representative characteristic of Greek education disappeared entirely from the schools of the Middle Ages. The liberal arts had no place for physical training. In our modern schools in the United States we provide for a modicum of physical education, but it remains very nearly an extracurricular activity. Thinking has become separate from physical activity. As Dewey expressed it, there occurred "the divorce of philosophy from life, the isolation of reflective theory from practical conduct." It is, he says, an "irony of history that this sudden and effective outcome was the result of the attempt to make thought the instrument of action, and action the manifestation of truth reached by thinking" (1897/1977, p. 57) While experimental procedures in the sciences have brought some reconciliation between physical activity and thinking, our underlying bias remains. Thinking is seen as a mental, not a physical, activity.

Just as the emphasis on literacy de-emphasized physical training, it also transformed music. What had been a family of activities that developed habits of grace, proportion, generosity, and courage through harmony, rhythms, and stories became a study of practical techniques for embellishing oratory. The musical study that Socrates encouraged—to "seek out the numbers" of harmonic intervals—was embraced in "the common medieval definition that 'music has to do with numbers as related to sounds'" (Theodore C. Karp, in Wagner, 1983, p. 174). Music as artistic creation and aesthetic experience was largely ignored. Medieval scholars of music "fostered a division between the senses and the mind, and precedence was given to the mind" (Karp, in Wagner, 1983, p. 177). As the senses are part of our physical life, this perspective reinforces the view that thinking is not a physical activity. And it adds a new limitation to thinking: Thinking is not affective. It is not concerned with our emotional responses to experience, and it is not expressed in aesthetic creation.

With the changes in the role of music in education, the element of "music" that Socrates calls "poetry" became increasingly dependent on literacy, and it moved to the provinces of the grammar teacher and literature teacher. As early as Protagoras, the study of poetry is described in terms of "the ability to understand the words of the poets, to know when a poem is correctly composed and when not, and to know how to analyze a poem and to respond to questions about it" (339a). The rhetorical study of poetry reflects the scholastic flavor of thinking: Knowing the vocabulary and answering questions are what we do with poems in classrooms. This rhetorical approach also reinforces the view that thinking is not affective. To comment on the beauty of a poem (as Socrates does when discussing an ode by Simonides in the dialogue *Protagoras*) is irrelevant to the sort of thinking that Protagoras is teaching about.

With the emergence of the liberal arts as templates of what a discipline is supposed to be, the liberal or general-education claims for the disciplines were promoted, and the separation of thinking from professional instruction and practice was reinforced. The disciplines were the domain of abstract mental endeavors rather than everyday practical affairs, arithmetic as number theory rather than arithmetic in banking and trade. This echoed Socrates' concern about studying mathematics for the purposes of "buying and selling," but without his perspective on the sort of instruction that befits a "liberal" study. Scholastic thought and teaching (in the tradition of Martianus Capella) was employed in the service of supposedly liberal aims. The rejection of turning general education (the liberal arts) to practical account thus came with an ironic twist: The liberal arts themselves became the profession of scholarship, and thinking became the basic tool of academia, the province and marker of the academic.

When the arts (with their pagan heritage) were turned to the service of Christian education, a new restriction was put upon thinking. Thinking was now trumped by faith:

Awareness that sanctification—the introjection of the Holy Spirit—came by God's action limited the confidence that the Fathers could place in human arts, including the art of scriptural interpretation. The sense of ultimate dependence upon God brought with it praise of holy simplicity, and of its paradigms—the illiterate fishermen who became apostles. . . . Holiness and erudition were neither mutually exclusive nor identical; but holiness had the greater weight (Karl F. Morrison, in Wagner, 1983, p. 52).

The Christian era was not the first time that the authority of thinking had been limited by the authority of faith—Socrates was put to death for the questions he asked!—but the Christian perspective on thinking reinforced the scholasticism of thought. A medieval scholar like Pierre Abelard could find a place for his theological use of the tool of rhetoric only in the schools (as the heresy charge against him affirmed). Thinking was bounded on one side by practical life, on the other by religious revelation.

A final dimension of the notion of thinking that emerged through the transformation of the Greek *paideia* into the medieval liberal arts is perhaps the most entrenched of all: The liberal arts (curricula) are external to the student. Almost 1,500 years after Martianus, Dewey expressed the problem this way: "We get the case of the child *vs.* the curriculum; of the individual nature *vs.* social culture. Below all other divisions in pedagogic opinion lies this opposition" (1902/1990, p. 183). The belief that the child is not only separate from but also, in some ways, in opposition to the curriculum follows naturally from the transformation of education that Marrou (1964, p. xiv) calls "the progressive transition from a 'noble warrior' culture to a 'scribe' culture." In the "noble warrior" culture, education in physical training and music sought to develop the child in body and soul. The activities of education could not be imagined as something separate from the children who ran and jumped and wrestled, who marched and sang. But in the "scribe" culture, the arts—of grammar, rhetoric, and dialectic; of arithmetic, geometry, astronomy, and music—represent the achievements of a culture, not the dimensions of individual nature. Today the list of disciplines is different—English grammar and composition, algebra, geometry, biology, world history, and all the rest—but the assumption remains that these achievements of the culture are not a natural outgrowth of "forces operating in the child's life," but rather that "there is some kind of gap in kind (as distinct from degree) between the child's experience and the various forms of subject-matter that make up the course of study" (Dewey, 1902/1990, p. 189). The child, it is felt, can only master these disciplines through the exercise of discipline—by the child to some degree, but even more so by the teacher and the administrators of the school, who must coerce the child to receive the curriculum.

When the curriculum is external to a child's life, non-thinking becomes almost inevitable. With "the tendency to isolate intellectual matters till knowledge is scholastic, academic, and professionally technical" comes "the widespread conviction that liberal education is opposed to the requirements of an education which shall count in the vocations of life" (Dewey, 1916/1966, p. 136). That which is called "thinking" in the school is seen as sterile, cut off from action, lacking in feeling, and of importance only to the academician. When the curriculum is external to a child's life, "intelligence is not adequately engaged" (p. 135). In fact, intelligence cannot be engaged, because the separation of the arts from the vocations of life deprives them of their meaning. The student encounters Shakespeare, cell structure, geometric proofs, and the causes of World War I; but the student does not know why except that this is what school requires. Thinking about these alien worlds is an impossibility.

So these are some of the ways in which thinking has been shaped by the transition of the Greek *paideia* into the medieval liberal arts and on into the curricula of our modern schools. All this is not to say that these influences are destiny or that there has been no resistance to these ways of thinking about thinking. In Chapter 1 I discussed efforts to classify affective and physical outcomes of instruction and to expand the concept of intelligence to include physical, musical, and interpersonal performances. These efforts and others like them (some as early as the writings of Saint Augustine) testify to an awareness of the need to resist and restructure the ways in which our historical legacy has characterized thinking. But of course this testimony merely shows that the legacy does exist and that it has restricted (and continues to restrict) how we think about thinking.

PART II

The Paradox of Telling

CHAPTER 3

The Content of Stories

Teachers tell students things.

In one of its starkest incarnations, this commonplace of schooling becomes Charles Dickens's "man of realities," Thomas Gradgrind, who instructs teachers as narrowly and directly as he would have them instruct children:

> "Now, what I want is Facts. Teach these boys and girls nothing but Facts. Facts alone are wanted in life. Plant nothing else, and root out everything else. You can only form the mind of reasoning animals upon Facts: nothing else will ever be of any service to them. This is the principle on which I bring up my own children, and this is the principle on which I bring up these children. Stick to Facts, sir!" (Dickens 1981/1854, p. 25).

Before Dickens is done with him, Gradgrind finds that his son, raised on the principle of the supremacy of Facts, has turned to crime. The son explains the felony to his father as a simple Fact of cosmic inevitability: A certain percentage of people put into positions of trust will abuse the trust. How can the father be so surprised? Gradgrind, his principle of life thrust so rudely in his face, imagines himself in old age "making his facts and figures subservient to Faith, Hope, and Charity; and no longer trying to grind that Heavenly trio in his dusty little mills" (p. 300).

The morality tale of Thomas Gradgrind epitomizes the dilemma of "telling." No one—certainly not Dickens—would argue that teachers should not teach facts to students. His lesson is rather that facts (or even Gradgrind's capital-letter "Facts") are not enough. Love and loyalty, forgiveness and regret, and mercy and understanding also help to form the mind of reasoning animals. But this insight, far from releasing teachers from the necessity of telling students things, seems to require even more "telling" and to reveal the hazards of telling the wrong things or of failing to tell the right ones.

Gradgrind has assumed that by filling his son with Facts, he would be ensuring that his son would think clearly and well, that the son would see the world as the father sees it and would act in ways the father would approve of. Instead, Gradgrind's industrious inculcation of Facts perverts and destroys thinking.

So here is the second paradox of thinking in classrooms: Teachers tell students things—facts, procedures, algorithms, histories, theories, myths—in order to help them think deeply, clearly, and wisely. Schooling requires this "telling," and thinking would be impoverished, and probably impossible, without it. But teachers cannot tell students everything. And there is a deeper dimension of the paradox: If students are told what they need to know, they don't need to think. The problem for the educator is to discover both when telling is unavoidable and when it leads to a deflection or undermining or perversion of thinking. In this chapter and the following, I explore the paradox of telling.

READING A STORY WRONG

In 1938 James Thurber wrote a short short-story called "The Macbeth Murder Mystery." The story consists of two brief conversations between the narrator and an inveterate reader of murder mysteries, the latter known simply as "the American woman." She happens to have read Shakespeare's *Macbeth* (because she picked it up by mistake), and she tells the narrator how much it disappointed her. "In the first place, I don't think for a moment that Macbeth did it." When the perplexed narrator asks, "Did what?" she replies, "I don't think for a moment that he killed the King. . . . I don't think the Macbeth woman was mixed up in it, either."

Her reasoning for this surprising conclusion makes perfect sense (from the point of view of the early-20th-century whodunit): "You suspect them the most, of course, but those are the ones that are never guilty—or shouldn't be, anyway. . . . It would spoil everything if you could figure out right away who did it. Shakespeare was too smart for that. I've read that people never *have* figured out 'Hamlet,' so it isn't likely Shakespeare would have made 'Macbeth' as simple as it seems."

The American woman goes on to explain her theory that Macduff did it. She points out that Macduff discovered the body. "Then he comes running downstairs and shouts, 'Confusion has broke open the Lord's anointed temple' and 'Sacrilegious murder has made his masterpiece' and on and on like that." The American woman sees through this ploy: "You wouldn't say a lot of stuff like that, offhand, would you—if you had found a body?"

She can even explain why Macbeth and Lady Macbeth try to "take the rap." Suspecting each other, they attempt to shield each other. The entire theory, with all its textual evidence, causes the narrator (and perhaps the reader as well) to feel that he has never really read the play before.

If we think of reading as a transactional activity in which the reader contributes to the creation of the work of art (in the spirit of John Dewey [1934/1980] and Louise Rosenblatt [1978]), the effect of Thurber's sketch of the American woman can be seen as a reminder of the ways in which habits of mind structure what we perceive. Read enough murder mysteries and we begin to see everything as an example of the genre. But Thurber's story also presents a different sort of lesson, one that leads into the problem of this chapter: The humor of the sketch derives from the fact that the woman misunderstands *Macbeth*. She reads it wrong. She is just as mistaken as if she asserted that the play was a grocery list, a restaurant menu, or a chronicle of the Mongol dynasty in China.

But how is it possible to read a text *wrong*?

The woman is clearly thinking about *Macbeth*, and thinking about it in a highly original way. She is attending to the text and quoting passages to support her reading. If she were to take a test about the facts of the play (Who are the characters? How are they related to one another? What do they say? What events are portrayed in what order?), she would easily pass the test. She is (we can assume) accurately reporting the nature of her encounter with the play. Where is the error?

The significance of this question is far greater than may seem possible at first glance. While some might say that because the example seems so unlikely the problem can be ignored, most teachers have encountered students who could read the words of an assignment without quite getting the point. Thurber's example is exaggerated for the sake of humor, but the problem is real.

Others might want to acknowledge the question as real, but dismiss it as trivial. This too seems to me to be a mistake. If educators accept as inconsequential the possibility that efferent reading (reading for information in a text) is unrelated to aesthetic reading (reading for engagement with a text), it becomes likely that assignments in their classrooms will tend to ignore aesthetic reading and to be reduced to the transcription of information—the essence of non-thinking.

So I want to take seriously the problem of the "American woman." This woman's reading of *Macbeth* is not the sort of thinking I want to encourage in school, and to explain my discomfort with her read-it-any-way-you-like approach, I have to answer what turns out to be a difficult question: How is it possible for her to quote *Macbeth*, to read the play so closely and so accurately, and yet to read it wrong? The kind of error Thurber's story points to is not a question of misrepresenting statements in the text or of mistaking the identity of the text. So what does it mean to say that a student reads something wrong?

If the puzzle of seeing a Shakespearean tragedy as a murder mystery seems to have little to do with non-thinking in classrooms, consider this: When a teacher presents her students with a text (whether this is a passage in a textbook, a video, a Web site, or her own personal retelling of subject matter), she is telling them she wants them to enter the world of that text. Entering that world—embracing what the reading has to offer—requires yielding to the text. And while seeing a text on its own terms in some ways enables thinking, it also removes possibilities. At least, this is the case I will be making in this chapter. I begin my attempt to unravel the question "What does it mean to say that a student reads something wrong?" by turning to the nature of stories.

THE LESSONS STORIES TEACH

Human societies have generally taken it for granted that stories teach lessons. From the fables of Aesop and parables of Jesus to McGuffey's readers and William Bennett's *Book of Virtues*, Western civilization has been steeped in edifying stories. Oral and literary storytelling have similarly shaped non-Western civilizations, with oral traditions playing a central role in the lives and cultures of indigenous peoples around the globe.

There is an implicit assumption underlying all this storytelling: Certain stories are good for people. There are, of course, debates about which stories are the good ones. Some people will argue that high-school students should, for example, read Shakespeare's *Macbeth* for the probing questions it asks about the meaningfulness of life. Others resent a "canon" of "dead, white males" and question whether this play speaks to high-school students at all. For my purposes, the important point is that almost everyone believes that there are some worthwhile stories (perhaps in the form of a movie rather than a book, a dialogue rather than a monologue, or being hypertextual rather than linear). The debates are not about whether stories teach lessons but rather about which lessons ought to be taught. In general, all agree that lessons—meanings—are embedded in stories. Supporters and opponents of "the canon" acknowledge that texts and pictures contain content that is in some way, to some degree, sufficiently fixed to be the medium for communicating a certain worthy (or unworthy), identifiable (though perhaps not definable) lesson. This point merits repeating: The implicit assumption is that the meaning (or meanings) of the story or the value (or values) to be shared by reading the story (in some way, to some degree) is *there* in the text. The thing-told retains meaning that transcends the lives of any set of tellers and hearers.

But why am I so concerned with stories? If this part of the book deals with how telling contributes to non-thinking in schools, what about all the other sorts of telling that teachers engage in? What about commands, rules, advice, criticisms, admonitions, instructions, procedures, algorithms, information? For, despite John Dewey's familiar warning that "education is not an affair of 'telling' and being told," children's experience in schools is saturated with these kinds of telling (1916/1966, p. 38).

I prefer to explore the problem of telling by looking at stories because, if this case can be made, readers can easily extend the argument to all the other forms of telling in schools. When the ways in which stories encourage non-thinking become clearer, the limitations on thinking can be recognized in other forms of telling that are more directive or didactic than narrative is. Also, it is arguable that narrative is the fundamental way in which we human beings structure our experience (see Doyle & Carter, 2003). Stories comprise a repository of wisdom, ideal, virtue, and faith. Storytelling is our primary form of telling. Teachers tell stories when they deal with the American Revolution, the Big Bang, photosynthesis, the structure of musical compositions, the fall of the Roman Empire, the paintings of Claude Monet, the causes of economic recession, the nature of gravity, forms of government, the water cycle, the effects of television on social life, and the uses of algebra.

But even if these arguments are compelling for looking at stories and storytelling, I may seem to have made a category error when I say that I look at stories to learn more about how thinking is influenced by the fact that teachers tell students things. Aren't stories more a matter of "showing" than of "telling"? More a matter of expression than of statement? It will be worthwhile to look at the traditional distinctions between telling and showing before trying to answer the question of how one can read a story wrong.

TELLING AND SHOWING

On the face of it, the difference between showing and telling is so obvious that kindergartners can understand it. When a child shows the puppet she brought to class for show-and-tell, she holds it up for everyone to see it. When she tells about the puppet, she says words. When someone shows something, we see it for ourselves; we have our own experience. When someone tells us something, we hear her version of her experience.

To characterize this distinction, John Dewey uses the terms *statement* and *expression*. A statement, says Dewey, is like a "signboard" that "directs one's course to a place, say a city. It does not in any way supply experience of that city." What the signboard does, he says, "is to set forth some of the conditions that must be fulfilled in order to procure that experience." A statement is "good" or "effective" if it "can be used as *directions* by which one may arrive at the experience" (1934/1980, p. 84). If the telling part of the show-and-tell is effective, the words the girl says will help her classmates imagine the experience the girl has with her puppet. Her words *state* a meaning, with the intention of guiding her classmates to discover a similar meaning in an experience of their own, but the words do not (unless the girl is a gifted storyteller) *express* a meaning.

Dewey wants to distinguish between statement and expression because this distinction illustrates the fundamental nature of experiencing art. "Science states meanings; art expresses them" (p. 84). Being in the presence of paintings and symphonies, movies and rock concerts, is not the same as being told about them—regardless of how insightful or explanatory the summaries or critiques are. Reading Dickens's *David Copperfield* or watching a performance of *Macbeth* is not the same as reading the Cliffs Notes version. The novel and the play express meaning, rather than stating it. The notes state meaning, rather than expressing it. Stories, it would seem, express or show, rather than state or tell. And if that is the case, if I want to look at teachers telling students things, I should ignore stories, which seem (from this analysis) not to be an instance of telling at all.

Now, those who have spent any time in classrooms will likely be thinking at this point that the tendency to take a Cliffs Notes perspective on literature must surely be part of the problem of non-thinking. Katherine Simon, for example, begins her book *Moral Questions in the Classroom* by recalling how she once taught *Macbeth*, focusing on the elements and structure of the play, dealing in statements about the play, rather than seeking to help students appreciate what the play expressed to them. This aspect of non-thinking will be reserved, however, for the following chapter. My concern here is with how the experience of expressiveness itself influences thinking and non-thinking.

The immediate question at issue is this: When a teacher asks students to read, say, Langston Hughes's "Ballad of the Landlord," is the teacher showing or telling? Or, to put it another way, what does the teacher expect the students to do to or with the poem? The instinctive response (the kindergartner's point of view) will be to say that the teacher is showing a poem to her class. In Dewey's language, she is inviting them to discover the meanings that the poem expresses. In Louise Rosenblatt's language, she is asking them to read aesthetically rather than efferently. Each of these terms (*show, express, aesthetic*) points toward experiencing the poem as a work of art capable of moving a reader to feel, to ponder, to see anew. As John Ciardi puts it, the aim is "to experience the poem as a poem" (1959, p. 667).

Suppose, though, that instead of a sixth-grade language arts class, the setting is an undergraduate teacher-education class. This time the teacher asks her students to read, in Jonathan Kozol's *Death at an Early Age*, Kozol's description of his introducing his students to Hughes's "Ballad of the Landlord." Here too the teacher wants her students to feel, to ponder, to see anew. Is this also an instance of showing? This situation seems less clear cut than that of the sixth-graders reading Hughes's poem. After all, *Death at an Early Age* is a work of nonfiction that is supposed to inform readers. It states meanings. The teacher who assigns the book probably intends it to be read efferently.

It may seem trivial to fret about whether to call an assignment a matter of "showing" or of "telling," and if it were simply a vocabulary question, it *would* be trivial. What is at issue, however, is why teachers ask students to read this instead of that, how it is (or what it means to say) that someone read a story wrong, and how the experience of expressiveness influences thinking and non-thinking.

The inadequacy of the commonplace distinction between showing and telling becomes clearer through looking at how Wayne Booth (1961) discusses the terms in his book *The Rhetoric of Fiction*. In brief, Booth sets out to dismantle the distinction between telling and showing. He argues that the attempt to rid novels of telling was a project that failed. Novelists and other storytellers cannot avoid telling. Every selection of words is inevitably a structuring of experience, an injection of stated meanings into an attempted reexpression of phenomenal existence.

As Booth tells it, the concern of novelists such as Gustave Flaubert and Henry James was that the quality of novels could be marred by the intrusion of the author into the tale. "Since Flaubert," says Booth (writing in the mid-20th century), "many authors and critics have been convinced that 'objective' or 'impersonal' or 'dramatic' modes of narration are naturally superior to any mode that allows for direct appearances by the author or his reliable spokesman" (1961, p. 8). A narrator who tells what events mean tells more than anyone can know. The result is that the author's version of reality is forced upon events or phenomena. This is, from the point of view of Flaubert, James, Anton Chekov, Jean-Paul Sartre, and others, bad storytelling because it is too much telling and not enough story, not enough showing.

Responding to this form of literary criticism, Booth counters that even a work in which the author is scrupulously absent presents a view of the world. "When the narrator judges," asks Booth, "how is the reader to avoid judging? To argue that the work simply intends to present a 'vivid picture' is meaningless, when the vivid picture consists of acts and statements which cannot be seen for what they are except in a setting of values" (1961, p. 382).

Here is how I understand the case Booth is making. First, the rhetorical skills of an author are used to re-create acts and statements that are shaped into a "vivid picture." But keep in mind what it is the author is working with: The author translates internal speech (that itself has been composed to represent reality, to stand in for an internal vivid picture of acts and statements) into an array of graphic symbols such as those printed on this page. The creation—if it succeeds, if a reader turns the symbols back into meaningful speech—is not a visual display of artistically arranged symbols, but rather acts and statements that form a vivid picture. The relationship between the reader's vivid picture and the author's creation is treated in the second element of the argument, which says that what the author crafts is meaningful only within a moral context, only from the perspective of the implied author— the creator of the voice that is speaking the text, the inventor of the storyteller. To see the acts and statements "for what they are" (some sort of match between the implied author's imputed vivid picture and the reader's emerging vivid picture) we readers *must* see the world as it is constructed by the implied author. This leads to a conclusion—namely, that the acts and statements an author records are *some*-thing. They may be open to endless interpretation, but they are not *any*-thing. It is possible to see them "for what they are" and therefore also possible to see them wrong.

Putting this argument back into the context of telling and showing, Booth's case says that telling cannot be separated from showing, because whenever we use words (or for that matter, paints or musical notes), we are dealing not in acts and statements themselves, but rather in symbolic representations of acts and statements. Telling is itself a kind of showing. This is why Dewey (1934/1980) says that "men in general are not aware that they have been exercising an art as long as they engaged in spoken intercourse with others" (p. 240). The act of speech is the practice of an art.

> The grandam [sic] telling stories of "once upon a time" to children at her knee passes on and colors the past; she prepares material for literature and may be herself an artist. The capacity of sounds to preserve and report the values of all the varied experiences of the past, and to follow with accuracy every changing shade of feeling and idea, confers upon their combinations and permutations the power to create a new experience, oftentimes an experience more poignantly felt than that which comes from things themselves (pp. 240–241).

It is important to be clear here that Dewey and Booth are approaching the question of "telling and showing" or "statement and expression" from the point of view of different problems. Booth is exploring the ways in which *authors* use telling and showing in their literary creations. He wants to demonstrate that skillful authorial commentary does not diminish aesthetic experience and that authors necessarily intermingle telling and showing in ways that blur the distinction between the two. Dewey, by contrast, is exploring the ways in which all of us experience statement and expression. He wants to demonstrate that while the experience of a text-as-statement is different from the experience of text-as-expression, we cannot neatly divide texts (or speeches, paintings, or events) into the categories of statement and expression. It is the reader's interaction with the text that finally determines if the commentary is aesthetic or if the words are merely a signpost.

So, whether we look at the author's task or the reader's task, we see a merging or overlapping of telling and showing. Ordinary language does not mislabel the activity when it speaks of "storytelling." We do *tell* stories, but we also expect them to *show* something. That is, we expect the telling to lead us to experience a world constructed according to the vision of an implied author. We expect the story to show us *some*-thing.

The next step toward understanding how someone can read a story wrong is to look more closely at this expectation.

SHOWING SOME-THING

Dewey teaches us (in ways that Rosenblatt expanded upon as she developed reader response theory) that whether a text (book, painting, symphony, event, garden scene contemplated from the backyard deck) is statement or expression depends upon the nature of the transaction between the "viewer" and the "text." Even instrumental music, which is often thought to be necessarily expressive, can become statement. The playing of "Pomp and Circumstance," the wedding march from *Lohengrin*, or "The Star-Spangled Banner" may be more like the signpost Dewey talks about than like the experience of the city. The music may simply serve to point us toward the graduates, or the bride, or the start of a baseball game.

Booth adds to this argument by teaching us how the response is constrained by the text. At a graduation ceremony I may not hear "Pomp and Circumstance" as if it preserves and reports "values of all the varied experiences of the past" or as if it creates a new experience "more poignantly felt than that which comes from things themselves." The performance may be perfunctory, the hall noisy, and the music simply a signpost that directs my attention to the graduates. But if I listen to "Pomp and Circumstance" and report that it brings to life all the horrors of the Nazi siege of Leningrad during World War II, something is wrong. If the orchestra really is playing "Pomp and Circumstance" (and not Shostakovich's 7th Symphony), I am not responding to what is being played; I am not hearing the notes "for what they are."

Occasionally in some of the classes that I teach I have demonstrated this. I play several pieces of music (a selection from "Century Rolls" by contemporary composer John Adams, a Sousa march, a Chopin étude, a set of Renaissance dances by Praetorius) and ask the students to draw a picture inspired

by the music or to write a list of words that come to mind. I then show one
of the pictures to the class or read one of the lists of words and ask which
piece of music is being described. Even when the students are unfamiliar with
the music, and I tell them nothing about the music, they are usually able (about
65% of the time in my trials) to identify which picture or which list of words
goes with which piece of music. A glance at the picture or list of words is
often enough to identify instantly which piece of music was the inspiration.
Almost never are the guesses random; certain selections seem to be immediately eliminated as possibilities. Pictures and word lists inspired by a Sousa
march have never in my trials been mistaken for those inspired by a Chopin
étude. The styles of John Phillip Sousa and of Frédéric Chopin are so distinctive that a list of words describing the march simply does not fit the étude.
Consider the following two lists composed by graduate students in one of
my trials. Which is Chopin and which is Sousa?

Patriotic	Falling
Carnival	Roller coaster
Carefree	Gently rolling
Concert	Calm before the storm
Happy	Death

On one occasion when I tried this activity, I used Claude Debussy's "Claire
de Lune," a piece called "L'orage" (The storm) by Norbert Burgmüller, and a
Johann Sebastian Bach Invention (No. 2). As might be expected, many of the
pictures drawn in response to "Claire de Lune" (music that *was* familiar to
most of the participants) were outdoor scenes with notable streaks of light.
All the pictures drawn in response to "L'orage" portrayed a storm, with several featuring a bolt of lightning that was traced back (in the ensuing discussion) to a particular passage in the music. In response to intentionally
programmatic music, such similarities may seem unremarkable. And in fact,
the pictures drawn in response to the Bach Invention were much more diverse.
One young woman drew a picture of Jesus on the cross because, she said,
"That's what the music made me think of." Nevertheless, the Bach-inspired
pictures were as easy to identify as were the pictures of the thunderstorm.
     This achievement is so commonplace that we may tend to overlook its
significance. Obviously a brass band sounds nothing like a solo piano. But
the pictures do not portray band or piano, and the lists of words do not
mention instrumentation. When my students identify the piece of music, what
they are matching up is their own experience listening to the music and the
stylistic elements of the music.
     When I talk about a composer's style, what I mean is that the music
consists of features that identify the music (to those who have studied such

matters) as belonging to a particular composer or period. The same sort of thing can be said, of course, about writers, speakers, painters, and teachers whose texts, speeches, paintings, and lessons are similarly identifiable by their style. Nelson Goodman says that "stylistic properties help answer the questions: who? when? where?" (1978, p. 34) Arguing that it is a mistake to suppose that style is simply a matter of *how* a work says what it says, Goodman insists that every aspect of a work's function as a symbol that helps to fix the work's identity is an aspect of style. "Basically," he says, "the style consists of those features of the symbolic functioning of a work that are characteristic of author, period, place, or school" (p. 35). The significance of this characterization in terms of author, period, place, or school is that it "informs the way the work is to be looked at or listened to or read" (p. 38).

I want to take a closer look at Goodman's claim that style is a matter of the "symbolic functioning of a work." Understanding why this is so helps to explain the expectation that stories show *some*-thing; and this explanation will, in turn, lead finally to an answer to the question of how it is possible (or what it means to say) that someone can read a story wrong.

Now, how does style come to be a matter of the "symbolic functioning of a work"? An example may help. Suppose I listen to an unfamiliar piece of music and say to myself, "That sounds like Tchaikovsky." What am I doing? Am I noticing that a large symphonic orchestra is playing, that the melodic line is singable and rather long, that scales are used prominently in the harmony?

As I reflect upon my response to music, what I find is that such pronouncements are not part of my first response to the music, even if these are precisely the ways that Peter Ilyich Tchaikovsky's style is usually described. What's wrong is that I *feel* the style before I *recognize* it. I respond to the work as an act of communication—as symbolic functioning—before I have analyzed the features that characterize its style. I feel the texture of the orchestra before I find the term to classify the orchestra. I feel the flow of the melody before I can say that it is long and singable. I am swept up by a rising emotion before I trace the feeling back to the scales in the harmony. When I was 18 years old and listened to Tchaikovsky's Sixth Symphony for the first time, I felt the quality of the experience even though I did not know the style of Tchaikovsky's music and probably could not have precisely pointed to the elements of the music that were responsible for what I was feeling. All I knew was that the music moved me and that, in ways I could not clearly explain, it reminded me of Chekov's *Cherry Orchard*. I wondered if the proximity of the two works in time and space signified a general mood presaging the end of the Romanov dynasty in Russia.

The significance of these adolescent musings is that they portray the effects of symbolic functioning. Just as lines on a page (if they are artistically arranged, if they bear the mark of an implied author worth listening to) can become "acts and statements," so too, combinations of sounds (if they are artistically arranged) can embody and convey experience. The reason we are able (with more exposure to works) to classify them by "author, period, place, or school" is that we have memorable, meaningful experiences that are exemplified by and embodied in stylistic features. Johannes Brahms and Gustav Mahler, like Tchaikovsky, wrote some long and singable melodies scored for large symphonic orchestras, but their music does not sound like Tchaikovsky's because it embodies and conveys different experiences. The shorthand used to describe musical style (long melody, symphonic orchestra) identifies which features to look for in a musical score or to listen for in a performance, but it cannot tell what the style means to a listener. Style may be in some ways quantifiable, but it is also qualitative. Nothing that is strictly quantifiable and devoid of symbolic functioning can be style. While the composer's signature at the top of the score clearly serves to identify the author, period, place, and school, it is not a matter of style, because it serves no purpose in a listener's experience of the music. A painter's signature on a canvas, however, may be a matter of style, as it could be perceived as an element of the composition (cf. Goodman, 1978, p. 35).

But how, then, does a listener, reader, or observer determine which features of a work to pay attention to or how to attend to them? Should the visitor to the art gallery analyze or ignore the frames around the pictures? Is the movement of the conductor's baton part of the performance of the symphony or irrelevant to it? Should the lines of all of the characters in *Macbeth* be trusted? Or should the reader believe that sometimes, some of the characters are lying? And if so, which ones? And when?

To answer these questions I want to consider another example. A few years ago one of my students quoted the following lines in a paper, noting that she did not recall who had written them.

> I have been one acquainted with the night.
> I have walked out in rain—and back in rain.
> I have outwalked the furthest city light.

I have to confess that I did not recognize the lines—that is, I could not recall ever having read the poem—but I was certain that I knew the poet, and after a quick Internet search, I found it.

Several stylistic features of the stanza can be enumerated. To begin with, it *is* a stanza, a portion of a narrative. It uses simple rhyme and simple vocabulary. It uses repetition of words and is written in the first person. The verse is written in sentences, and the sentences are short and uncomplicated.

More notable (perhaps) than these surface features is the turning to nature. The poet talks about night and rain and about leaving the city.

I don't believe, however, that any of these were the first thoughts that occurred to me when I read this unattributed stanza in the student's paper. My first thought was that it was lazy of the student not to find the author. Such things can be easily discovered, and it may be (I thought) that knowing the author would affect how the lines should be read. My second thought was that this unattributed stanza was a challenge to me, and I was determined to identify it.

Even this sequence of events may not be precisely correct, however, because by the time I thought of taking up the challenge, I was already reasonably certain who the author was, and it wasn't because of any of the features of the stanza I enumerated above. Or, at least, it wasn't because of any of them as presented in that unsymbolic manner. It may have been because of all of them, but only because all of them tacitly worked together to tell me something about the speaker. The voice of the poem (Booth's "implied author") is a plain speaker who relishes the less traveled path. I was sure it had to be Robert Frost (Frost, 1928).

Now, the significance of this example is that I didn't decide which features of the lines to pay attention to. To ask, "How does the listener, reader, or observer determine which features of a work to pay attention to?" assumes that we begin the perception of a work with a blank mind. We don't. We perceive a work only when (and because) it functions symbolically: It says something. Our initial awareness of the content—of what is being said— guides decisions about which features to pay attention to. Examination of the features extends, reinforces, reshapes, or questions the initial response. From my first reading of the lines, I felt that they sounded like Frost; later, I began to notice the markers that might account for that response. The diction, the simple first-person narrative, the tone of faint regret—these fit my experience with Frost; and they deepened the symbolic functioning of the work because the stylistic identification brought with it memories of "The Road Not Taken," "Stopping by Woods on a Snowy Evening," and "Fire and Ice."

If my examples (listening to Tchaikovsky and reading Frost) accurately typify the relationship between the symbolic functioning of a work and the stylistic features of a work, they reveal what may be a surprising conclusion: Reading the lines or hearing the notes "for what they are" cannot be reduced to surface features. We can know the lines so well that we can quote them from memory, paraphrase them, and translate them into another language, and still not be able to read them "for what they are." Any classification of the features of a work is an incomplete reading if it exclusively favors what the work "tells" and ignores what it "shows." We cannot recognize style if we fail to attend to (or misperceive) what a work expresses—even if we seem to master perfectly what the work states. And if we are oblivious to the style, we misunderstand and misread the work.

The need to be attentive to style doesn't mean, however, that first readings are empty of symbolic functioning, so that a student's first encounter with *Macbeth*, or "The Ballad of the Landlord," or Tchaikovsky's Sixth Symphony, calls for the teacher to prepare the student by focusing on the statement the work supposedly makes or on catalogs of surface features of the work. Even though the Sixth Symphony was my first encounter with Tchaikovsky, it spoke to me about melancholy and frustrated, hopeless passion (favorite themes of many 18-year-olds of that era). Even though "The Ballad of the Landlord" was the first encounter of Kozol's students with the poetry of Hughes, it spoke to them about the bitterness of their own lives. Both responses are instances of perception of style before the "reader" is capable of naming or classifying pertinent stylistic features. Neither a full analysis of a work's style nor classification of its period and genre is a prerequisite for responding to a work. In fact, it is the other way around: A reader or hearer must feel some response to a work before the style of the work can be discovered.

Yet, as Gardner insists, "knowledge of the origin of a work . . . informs the way the work is to be looked at or listened to or read." He is saying that knowing what sort of thing a work is supposed to be provides guidance for how one approaches the work. If I read a love letter as if it is a treatise on logic (as Abelard seems to do in his correspondence with Heloise), I will be less able to discover what Gardner calls the "nonobvious" features of the letter's style and less competent at refining my initial sense of the letter's symbolic functioning. Or, to put it more simply, I will fail to understand what my lover is saying.

When we say that a story is *some*-thing, we refer to more than a particular group of dark lines on a certain white page, more than the sentences and paragraphs those lines stand for, more even than the statements those sentences and paragraphs embody. What the "American woman" misses in her encounter with Shakespeare's *Macbeth* is what it feels like to lust for power so deeply that one would kill the king—and one's soul—to get it. Because she does not feel the play expressing Macbeth's world, she cannot recognize the play's style. Taking *Macbeth* to be a puzzle to be figured out, she concludes that the Elizabethan poetry, with its metaphoric flourishes ("Sacrilegious murder has made his masterpiece"), is simply "a lot of stuff" an ordinary person would not say without having planned it in advance. Without feeling for the tragedy in *Macbeth*, she doesn't know which features of the play to pay attention to. This is what it means to say that someone read a story wrong. The "American woman" cannot yield to *Macbeth*; she can only make the paperback in her hands yield to her.

THINKING ABOUT STORIES

The case I have made in the first half of this chapter can, of course, be disputed. From the perspective of postmodernism/structuralism/deconstruction (what Iris Murdoch [1993] calls "demythologization"), I have paid too much attention to the author (ignoring power relations embodied in the text) and have therefore given too much authority to the author. From the perspective of, say, E. D. Hirsch Jr., I have insufficiently emphasized the importance of the author's intentions and have therefore allowed too much latitude for variant readings. From both perspectives, concerns would likely be raised about an argument based on the necessity for a reader to respond to the transcendent expressiveness of a text. As Iris Murdoch has written, the notion of transcendent meaning or truth "has increasingly posed itself as a problem" in the past half century despite structuralism's "attack" on the "unified work of art" aiming at "the removal of the transcendent" (1993, pp. 2–5). And this problem is evident in the case I have made: If the "work" of art is the interaction of the reader or observer with the text, in what sense is the work *some*-thing that is stable and transcends any set of tellers and hearers of the story? Or even all my own experiences with the work?

As a way of (indirectly) addressing these questions, I want to turn to the instructional implications of the case I have made so far in this chapter. How might understanding what it means for students to read a story wrong affect what teachers do? How does experience with stories influence thinking and non-thinking?

To begin with, my case argues that if teachers are to avoid encouraging non-thinking, they must choose the stories they ask students to read (or watch or listen to) because of the experiences the story affords. To do this requires recognizing that just because a story can be read wrong, it need not follow that there exists a single, preordained, right reading (or experience) toward which a teacher must shepherd her students. As Wayne Booth says, "Most works worth reading have so many possible 'themes,' so many possible mythological or metaphorical or symbolic analogues, that to find any one of them, and to announce it as what the work is *for*, is to do at best a very small part of the critical task" (1961, p. 73). Finding the "lesson" or the "moral" of a story denies rather than embraces the experiences the story affords.

For example, to suppose (as William Bennett does in his *Book of Virtues*) that Alfred, Lord Tennyson's "Charge of the Light Brigade" teaches "responsibility" or that the story of George Washington and the cherry tree teaches "honesty" is deliberately to ignore the experiences that the poem and the story may afford.

Here is what Bennett says in his introduction to "The Charge of the Light Brigade":

> Some find it fashionable to ridicule this poem as a glorification of war and paean to those who blindly, and stupidly, follow orders. But the fact is that there are times when obedient acts of self-sacrifice and courage merit both admiration and profound gratitude. (1993, p. 221)

I find it a curious notion of responsibility to equate it with obedience. When people explain their actions by saying that they were following the orders or directions of someone in authority (that is, when they are obedient), they are saying that they are emphatically not responsible for their actions. Bennett's equation of obedience with responsibility makes a striking contrast to a line in the movie *Gandhi* in which Gandhi, discussing what the British can do to him if he insists on noncooperation, acknowledges that they can kill him, but, he says, "then they will have my dead body—not my obedience." In Gandhi's thinking (at least, that of the Gandhi in the movie), obedience is the antithesis of responsibility.

But discussions of the nature of responsibility, or of the ways in which the term *responsibility* is commonly used, are not to the point for my purposes in this chapter. What is significant about Bennett's introduction to "The Charge of the Light Brigade" is that it makes clear that he is not especially concerned with Tennyson's poem. It is the event—the obedient act of self-sacrifice and courage—that Bennett admires and urges others to admire as well. He is not suggesting that we should admire Tennyson for having created this poem, but rather that we admire the Light Brigade for having made their futile charge. Apart from establishing that a cavalry attack occurred and many were killed, Tennyson's poem is irrelevant to the lesson Bennett wishes to teach.

Suppose, however, we take a closer look at Tennyson's work. Here is perhaps the most famous stanza from that poem:

> "Forward, the Light Brigade!"
> Was there a man dismay'd?
> Not tho' the soldier knew
>   Someone had blunder'd:
> Theirs not to make reply,
> Theirs not to reason why,
> Theirs but to do and die:
> Into the valley of Death
>   Rode the six hundred.

The storytelling here involves more telling than showing. Tennyson tells us that the soldiers are doomed, that they perhaps know it, but that knowing it does not matter. We hear the command, and then the narrator speculates on the morale of the soldiers and tells us about their sense of duty, before picking up the refrain, "Into the valley of Death / Rode the six hundred."

In the next stanza the narrator offers more of a picture of the ill-fated charge:

> Cannon to right of them,
> Cannon to left of them,
> Cannon in front of them,
>   Volley'd and thunder'd;
> Storm'd at with shot and shell,
> Boldly they rode and well,
> Into the jaws of Death,
> Into the mouth of Hell,
>   Rode the six hundred.

The look of the cannon belching fire and steel, the sound of the horse's shrieks and the soldiers cries, and the smell of gunpowder and torn-open bodies are not portrayed in these lines; but there is a sketch of how the forces are arrayed, an estimate of the capacity for killing. The narrator tells us how the soldiers rode and calls upon an allusion to hell (perhaps a more frightening and evocative allusion in the 1850s than today) to elevate the sense of horror.

In the following two stanzas the narrator continues the description of the charge through the Russian battery and the retreat back to the British lines. The poem concludes with a shorter stanza in which the narrator states what this battle should mean to us readers and how we should feel about the characters of this story:

> When can their glory fade?
> Oh, the wild charge they made!
>   All the world wonder'd.
> Honor the charge they made!
> Honor the Light Brigade—
>   Noble six hundred!

This is presumably the key stanza for Bennett, as it states the "lesson" of the charge as Bennett sees it, and perhaps as Tennyson saw it as well. My problem with this reading is not, as Bennett suggests, that I want to ridicule the glorification of war (which is just another way of denying the experiences the poem affords), but rather that the exhortation in the final stanza cannot make me forget the echoes of the first stanza I quoted above. "Theirs

not to make reply, / Theirs not to reason why, / Theirs but to do and die."
The repetition of what it is not "theirs" to do is as confining and threatening
as the cannon to right, cannon to left, cannon in front. The proud young
men in their fancy uniforms live and die by a code of conduct they cannot
imagine questioning, but I question it, and I hope the young men and women
of today who read these lines question this code. I hope they ask if they too,
in their less dramatic lives of school and work, are denied the chance to make
reply or reason why, just as I hope they recognize that others have lived other
lives.

This brief response to Tennyson's poem is probably far different from
that of many other readers, but it illustrates what I mean when I call for teachers to evaluate stories for the experiences the story affords—for the story's
power to help readers (or listeners or viewers) to live larger lives. One of the
ways that teachers encourage non-thinking when they tell or present stories
is that, as Bennett does in this example from *The Book of Virtues*, they turn
attention away from the text (and any experiences it affords) toward a dis-
tilled "lesson," supposedly embedded in the story but yet separate from it.
Louise Rosenblatt describes this as "the naïve tendency to think of works of
literary art as made up of a literal sense, to which 'poetic' or 'literary' overtones can be added" (1978, p. 96).

This tendency, probably shared by many teachers, may be naive, but it
is certainly understandable, for it rests upon a convincing (if mistaken) analogy. When Bennett considers "The Charge of the Light Brigade" as a know-
able object, he assumes that it is comparable to, say, the Pythagorean theorem.
The poem, like the theorem, is intangible. The reasons for and implications
of this assumption will become clearer through looking at the other story I
mentioned from Bennett's anthology.

Bennett includes a telling of the story of young George Washington
chopping down his father's favorite cherry tree and then shamefully confess-
ing his crime, only to discover that his father valued George's honesty more
than he valued the cherry tree. Bennett does not comment on the irony that
an admittedly fictitious event is used to portray "honesty," nor does he say
anything about the particular version of the story he includes other than that
it is "an early twentieth-century rendition," and his indifference both to the
curiosity of fable masquerading as biography and to the special characteristics of the version of the story says a great deal. It doesn't matter whether it
is "Parson" Weems's original version of the tale or someone else's, because
the text is of no particular interest to Bennett. All that matters is the "literal
sense." For Bennett it is in the "literal sense" that the story possesses stabil-
ity. A version of the story from the early 19th century is equivalent to one
from the early 20th century presumably because both are seen as possessing
the same "literal sense." Both contain some common elements (young Wash-

ington, his ax, the cherry tree, and the father) and two events (the chopping down of the cherry tree and the confession); but even more important, both are understood to be vehicles of "honesty." While "literary overtones" can be added (the ax glints in the sun, or tears stream down George's face as he says, "Father, I cannot tell a lie"), these "literary" touches are irrelevant. Bennett ignores the style of the stories because he doesn't believe that the truth students are supposed to see lies in "literary overtones." He believes that the meaning lies elsewhere.

Bennett could make exactly the same sort of claim about the Pythagorean theorem. It doesn't matter whether the theorem is in Greek, Latin, or English. It can be stated as an equation or illustrated in a diagram. All these are equally valid versions of the Pythagorean theorem, and any of them is adequate if it conveys the idea of the theorem, if it conveys the "literal sense." An equation stating the theorem uses variables and operational signs in the same way that the George Washington story uses characters and events. And just as the theorem-in-itself (rather than any version of it) is an idea stating the eternal relationship of the imaginary lines that form ideal right triangles, the story of George Washington and the cherry tree states (for Bennett, at any rate) the eternal reality of the ideal of honesty. In the same way, it could be said that "The Charge of the Light Brigade" states the ideal of responsibility, and *Macbeth* the ideal of a misbegotten pride and lust for a power.

The argument I have made in this chapter does not disprove this perspective on stories and the way they work. I am not trying to prove that a story is, in some ontological sense, a different form of being from that of a mathematical theorem, because the issue is more psychological than ontological. We can choose to read, discuss, describe, and use stories any way we wish. I have argued, rather, that if we suppose that a story is like a theorem (so that the idea of the thing is all that matters and the form it takes—the style—can be safely ignored), we make it impossible to think about a story as a story. We forget that Shakespeare translated into Greek is not quite the same, just as Sophocles translated into English is not quite the same. We suppose that reading the Cliffs Notes version is pretty much the same as reading the original. We remove from consideration the features that make a story a distinct act of communication. If the specifics of the text are irrelevant, there is no longer an implied author who situates events from the stance of a particular view of the world. The significance of the story of George Washington and the cherry tree (from Bennett's perspective) does not derive from its authorship by Weems, just as the significance of the Pythagorean theorem does not derive from Pythagoras. Both story and theorem may be attributed to someone, but that is just a historical footnote, unconnected to the "literal sense." When the style of a story is seen as a temporary vehicle for the content of the story, a teacher does not need to ponder how the experiences a story affords are a product of the text created by an author; she can simply assert the truth the story is supposed to express.

A teacher who subscribes to this perspective turns attention away from the text and away from experiences afforded by the text, undermining the possibility of students' thinking about the stories told or presented to them. Even though such teachers emphasize a kind of engagement with the story and seek to make it meaningful, close attention to the text is not necessary. Pondering one's response and the features of the text that account for that response are precluded by the predetermined "lesson." When a teacher separates the study of style from the appreciation of meaning by emphasizing the "literal sense," she tells students that they need not consider the features of the text to understand what the work is about. This leads to non-thinking, because there is nothing left for students to think about.

The conceptual separation of style and symbolic functioning does not, however, always express itself as an emphasis on "literal sense." There is a second way that teachers sometimes encourage non-thinking when they tell or present stories: A story may be presented as an entirely open text to which students may respond in any way whatsoever. Where the examples from Bennett illustrate the belief that content ("literal sense") is fixed, and stories are merely vehicles in which it is transported, the open-text approach assumes that nothing is stable and that the content of a story is nothing more than what the reader makes of it.

Educationally, this approach is self-defeating, for it dissolves the concept of curriculum and, with it, the notion of teaching. If the act of thinking is all that is desired, with no concern for the content, means, or conclusions of the thinking, then, as Ewald Terhart has written,

> a non-subjectivist form of engagement with subject matter claims ceases to be possible. Instead of finding reasons, understanding, there can be only encounters; substance becomes process; engagement and further development of the achieved reservoirs of knowledge and experience would not then be possible. (2003, p. 38)

Still, the appeal of allowing students to find their own meaning in a text is strong, because it is the only way for a text to have any meaning. The non-thinking arises when, because of the separation of style and symbolic functioning, a teacher no longer has grounds on which to declare that a particular reading is wrong. In Thurber's story, the "American woman" is thinking, but she is not thinking about *Macbeth*. The teacher who cannot make the case for why this reading is wrong (a case that requires an interpretation of the interplay between style and symbolic functioning) leaves nothing for students to think about. *Macbeth* is then no longer *some*-thing stable that transcends any set of storytellers and hearers; it is just a name given to a family of readers' responses, some of which may show little if any family resemblance.

THE PROBLEM OF TELLING

Thus far I have argued that when a story is presented in a manner that separates style from symbolic functioning, non-thinking is encouraged either because the approach emphasizes "literal sense" or because it deprives a story of any sense at all. In the first instance, a predetermined meaning is imposed upon a story; in the second, the possibility of meaning dissolves because there is no such thing as a wrong reading. Either way, thinking about the story becomes pointless. Completing this argument requires acknowledging that the problem of telling does not vanish even when teachers seek to unify style and symbolic functioning and to emphasize the ways in which stories both show and tell, state and express, invite and control.

When we talk about a great book, a favorite movie, or a mesmerizing teacher, we often talk about getting lost in the experience. When telling becomes a work of art, it moves us beyond the object of contemplation and beyond ourselves. "The work of art," Dewey wrote, "tells something to those who enjoy it about the nature of their own experience of the world . . . it presents the world in a new experience which they undergo" (1934/1980, p. 83). Not only have we added something new to ourselves, but we find that the world as we used to see it has changed. By a curious twist, when we attend to the text and lose ourselves in the world of the "implied author," we discover that we are really thinking about the world in which we live. The story of an individual becomes the story of humankind. The story of Main Street becomes the story of the world. Louise Rosenblatt, reflecting on the power of a story not only to create a world but also to enlighten the reader's world, turns to an example from Shakespeare:

> Again, one marvels at how the story of a vain, authoritarian, quick-tempered old man like Lear can, by the end of the play, take on such dimensions that his fate seems not one man's tragedy but expressive of the human condition. Of course, reasons are to be sought in the text, the precise sequence of words found in the text—no mere summary of the play would have such an effect. . . . Shakespeare's text still must be seen as both controlling and yet open. (1978, p. 98)

Of course, we don't need to turn to "great literature" to see how the content of stories becomes the content of readers' lives. Discussing what she has learned through her study of the 19th-century children's magazine *The Youth's Companion*, literacy professor Laura Apol writes, "I have learned that children's literature creates a world that readers believe and shapes both individual and national memory" (2002, p. 59). At the beginning of her study, Apol explains, the stories of frontier life in the late 19th century led her to discover a "new understanding of the positioning power of text" that enabled her to help her students appreciate "the enormous ideological power that texts possess" (pp. 56–57). Her aim was to arm her students against the power of texts so that they could choose when to yield to the text, embracing its view of the world, and when to reject it.

But Apol's fear of the power of a text to control the reader began to undergo a surprising change as she explored the papers of an earlier scholar and discovered a cache of old letters from faithful readers of the magazine, letters written 50 years after the magazine had last been published. Reading about what the magazine had meant to its readers, Apol asked herself,

> How could I explain the kind of passion *The Youth's Companion* seemed to inspire in its readers? What would make a woman get up to sweep in the dark to earn a subscription to *The Companion*, or a man rush into a burning building to save his copies of the magazine? What would make a man remember for seventy-five years that he needed to know the outcome of a survival tale? What prompted [one reader] to spend his savings on a bus ticket [to see the site of a story], or to build a cabin across from the setting of an author's stories? (p. 58)

When Apol ponders these questions and examines her own excitement as she visits the building where the magazine had been published a century earlier, she concludes that the answer is

> [p]assion—the pull of a good story, the way a text can enter a reader's heart and stir feeling that leads to action: the action of sweeping a store in the dark or rushing into a burning house, buying a plot of land with a particular view or thrilling to see an old building decades after the presses have stopped. (p. 59)

Talking like this about how a "good story" enters a reader's heart and stirs feelings is nothing new, of course. What makes Apol's journey—both to the "old building" where *The Youth's Companion* was published and to a deeper understanding of the power of reading—interesting to me is that she is talking about stories that most people would dismiss as inconsequential. She herself was initially disappointed in them. She'd originally looked at *The Youth's Companion* because the magazine was published at a time when the reality of frontier life was changing women's lives. She'd hoped she would find in the magazine evidence of the ways in which "gender roles were being explicitly renegotiated" (p. 56). Instead, she found that the stories in *The Youth's Companion* "reinforced the rigid gender roles of the 19th century" (p. 56). Because of this disjunction between the world of the stories and the world of the 19th-century frontier, Apol became more aware of the ways in which stories control readers and better able to speak about the "positioning power of stories."

In the end, however, Apol does not dismiss *The Youth's Companion* as false consciousness or propaganda or inconsequential children's fare. She comes to feel that the power of the stories is (these are my words, not hers) not so much oppressive as it is enabling, not so much to deny truths as to give life. She knows that the stories are not what she wants them to be and not consonant with the lives she had read about in women's journals and diaries, and this doesn't matter, because the stories enter reader's hearts and stir their feelings to live lives that are more meaningful.

This is the power of stories that lies at the heart of the problem of telling. This is why Jean-Jacques Rousseau (in his part-novel, part-educational-treatise *Émile*) says he will postpone teaching Émile to read until the boy is at least 12. Rousseau wants Émile to think his own thoughts, not other people's thoughts. Rousseau understood that to experience a story, or to see the words "for what they are," requires us to yield to the story, to respond to the invitation of the implied author to enter and live in that author's world, to see as that implied author sees. Once we have done this, there is no going back. We cannot unsee what we have seen.

Rousseau's response to the danger that stories will infect the mind is (like Plato's) to restrict the stories to which the young may be exposed, but this seems a poor choice in our world. Children have hundreds of channels on their television sets and uncountable Internet sites on their computers. Their minds are already infected. What we need, paradoxically, is not *less* telling, but (at least, in schools) *more*. We need more telling if children are to learn to think about the stories they are told by all the voices—commercial, political, religious, educational—of our society and our world. We need more telling if children are to get beyond seeing a division between themselves and "others," if they are to overcome the tendency to "see only what their own minds have created, never the reality of the person who stands before them" (Nussbaum, 1997, p. 87).

Of course, when I say "more telling," I am talking about choosing stories for the experiences the stories afford. I am talking about treating them as stories, as the interplay of style and symbolic functioning. If students are to think about a story, they need to be allowed to respond to it in their own way, from their own understanding, but they also need to test that response against the text. If students are to think about a story, they need to know that it means nothing until they have entered its world, but they also need to accept that it is possible for them to read it wrong, which means having failed to enter that world. If students are to think well, they will need to have entered many worlds.

CHAPTER 4

Stories in Context

Some years ago I sat in a second-grade classroom, observing the children at work. One of the girls was sitting at a desk near me, solving some arithmetic problems, and after a while she approached me for help.

"I can't get this one," she said.

I read the problem, which said something like this: "Godzilla was smashing houses in Tokyo. He smashed seven houses with his right foot and eight houses with his left foot. How many houses did he smash all together?"

The problem didn't seem to me to be all that difficult for this second-grade class. The children had been adding one-digit numbers for some time, so I wondered why this question stumped the girl. I thought that perhaps she was unable to read the question, so I asked her to read it to me, which she did without any stumbling, hesitating, or misreading.

More puzzled than before, I made some conversation while I pondered how to help the girl. "Do you know who Godzilla is?" I asked.

"No."

"He's a monster in a lot of Japanese movies." I went on to describe from as best as I could recall the appearance of Godzilla (sort of a fire-breathing tyrannosaurus) and to mention some of his more notable battles. I dimly remembered that Godzilla defeated King Kong and an assortment of other monsters that threatened Earth (repeatedly). I think I said something about primitive special effects and about awkward dubbing from Japanese into English. Eventually the girl looked up at me and said, "OK, I've got it," and she went back to her seat and solved the arithmetic problem.

Over the years, I've told this story many times to students in my teacher education classes, perhaps because I'm still trying to figure it out. What had happened during my interaction with this child? How can I explain her sudden ability to solve an arithmetic problem—even though we had said nothing about arithmetic?

It seems likely to suppose that the girl had been unable to imagine the scene described in the story problem. The name Godzilla was an empty blank, and it created too big a hole in the problem for the problem to make any sense to her. This interpretation could be combined with arguments from Chapter 3, where I said that a meaningful encounter with a text begins with recognizing the symbolic functioning of the text. To read the problem, the girl has to create a "vivid picture," and she cannot create this picture unless she can supply some sort of image corresponding to the name Godzilla.

But while this interpretive reading of the event explains how the second grader came to appreciate the content of the story problem, it doesn't really explain what she did when she returned to her seat, or what she meant when she said, "OK, I've got it."

What exactly is it that she got?

In this chapter I'm going to argue that to understand how this second grader moved from envisioning Godzilla to writing the sum of 7 and 8, we have to turn our attention from the content of the story to its context. The teacher did not present the story problem to his class because he wanted them to contemplate an image of Godzilla. He presented the problem to the class because he wanted the children to acquire facility at adding numbers. He wanted his students to move from the content of the text (a minivignette in which a monster smashes houses) to the context of the text (the teacher has given these story problems to the second graders, and he expects them to turn in answers).

Our Godzilla story helps to illustrate the different influences on thinking and non-thinking of the content and the context of telling, and there are other reasons for using it to begin this chapter. Students are constantly encountering texts filled with Godzillas—filled, that is, with terms, phrases, and symbols they do not recognize. Concern about this fact of schooling and responses to it are currently driving educational policy, and they are driving it (as I will argue in this chapter) toward non-thinking by emphasizing what Philip Jackson has called "mimetic" teaching and what E. D. Hirsch Jr. has promoted as the "core knowledge" of "cultural literacy" (Hirsch, 1987; Hirsch, Kett, & Trefil, 2002; Jackson, 1986). Because the Godzilla story deals with a student who lacks some information and therefore cannot complete schoolwork, it seems to exemplify the problem that school critics such as Hirsch see as the weakness of American schooling. My intervention (telling the girl about Godzilla) then appears to be the fix for the problem. But this diagnosis and prescription misunderstand the Godzilla story and lead to the institutionalization of non-thinking. To explain why this is so, I want to look more closely at what Philip Jackson (1986) has called "mimetic" teaching and what I have called "teaching by the numbers" (Boostrom, 1997).

MIMETIC TEACHING

Teaching, says Philip Jackson, has been torn between two visions of what it is that teachers should try to accomplish. Those who have emphasized what Jackson calls "mimetic" teaching have focused on "the transmission of factual and procedural knowledge from one person to another" (1986, p. 117). Those who have emphasized what Jackson calls "transformative" teaching (he offers Socrates and Jesus as exemplars) have focused on bringing about "a qualitative change often of dramatic proportion, a metamorphosis" in the character and attitudes of students (p. 120). These two traditions of teaching have competed under many different names over the past few thousand years, and they continue to be defended by vigorous adherents, who are convinced that those who fail to see the virtues of the preferred tradition misunderstand the genuine nature of teaching and learning.

One such adherent, George Cunningham, expressing his dismay that the transformative, or progressive, perspective has (in his view, misguidedly) become entrenched in schools of education, illustrates the fervor and depth of righteous advocacy generated in defense of these conflicting traditions:

> There are two major competing philosophies in education. One asserts that teachers should focus on increasing their students [sic] academic achievement. The other dismisses the importance of academic achievement and instead defines good teaching as the creation of a classroom atmosphere that eschews explicit instruction in favor of giving responsibility for learning to the students. The two approaches are incompatible and there is really no way to create a compromise between the two. The question left unanswered is who gets to decide between the two. Legislatures, governors, and the federal government through NCLB [the No Child Left Behind Act] have declared that academic achievement should be paramount. The faculties of education schools and the national organizations that support them have decided otherwise. (2003)

On another occasion, Cunningham had expressed the message even more clearly in terms of warning and embattlement:

> Make no mistake about it. Education in America today is a battle between two cultures: the culture of progressive education and the culture of traditionalists who believe that all students should learn conventional curriculum at a high level. (2002)

As a defender of what Jackson calls the "mimetic" tradition, Cunningham feels that to question the merits of mimetic instruction is to misunderstand what teachers are supposed to do. He warns that progressive (or Jackson's "transformative") instruction shortchanges students. Even worse, those who battle on behalf of "the culture of progressive education" place themselves beyond the possibility of compromise or debate. These competing traditions cannot, says Cunningham, be reconciled through discussion. The supporters of one side or the other will be victorious. The issue is a political one, not an educational or philosophical one.

Cunningham's sense of urgency results, I believe, from his conviction that these two traditions of teaching are irreconcilable, an assertion that becomes more significant as it is examined more closely. How can the aims, procedures, and assumptions of the two traditions be so at odds as to preclude conversation? Both traditions involve teachers and students and subject matter. Both speak about such artifacts as schools, textbooks, tests, and curriculum guides. Yet Cunningham finds that he lives in a world so different from that of progressive, transformative teachers that he cannot talk to them in a way that acknowledges that both sides are, after all, working in the same field.

Toward the end of this chapter I'll return to this assertion of irreconcilability and argue that to understand why Cunningham feels this way helps to explain the significance of the Godzilla story for thinking and non-thinking. But to make this case, I need to say more about the mimetic tradition.

Jackson explains that he has selected the term *mimetic* because "it places the emphasis" where he believes "it belongs, on the importance of *method* within this tradition" (1986, p. 117). The method is direct and recognizable to anyone who has ever sat in a classroom. In Step 1, teacher tests the student, to see if the student "knows the material or can perform the skill in question" (p. 119). The teacher then, in Step 2, presents the material. This second step is probably what most people think of when they think of "teaching." In Step 3 the student performs and the teacher evaluates. In Step 4 the teacher either rewards and reinforces a correct performance or remediates an incorrect one. The sequence is completed in Step 5 with the student advancing to the next topic or skill.

Embedded in the mimetic tradition is a concept of knowledge that Jackson says "is familiar to most of us, though its properties may not always be understood" (p. 117). Knowledge as it is conceived within the mimetic tradition is always secondhand: It exists prior to the student's encounter with it. This is crucial because it supports the second step of the mimetic method, in which the teacher presents the material. Without some sort of predetermined knowledge, there is nothing for the teacher to present. Even if, outside the classroom, knowledge is being added to or rewritten, inside the classroom it exists (from the mimetic perspective) in a fixed, transmissible state.

This notion of knowledge as something preexistent and finished is so familiar that my students (who are themselves both experienced and preservice teachers) often have difficulty imagining a rival notion of knowledge in which it is not secondhand. For them, the transaction in which a student engages with a text and through which experience and meaning emerge (as discussed in Chapter 3) is typically not considered to be an instance of knowledge at all. They tend to see knowledge as it is understood within the mimetic tradition—presented, not constructed.

A second characteristic of knowledge within the mimetic tradition is that it is "detachable" (p. 118). This is knowledge that can be forgotten. It can be possessed for a time (often long enough to pass a test) and then wither away until little or nothing remains of what once had been "learned." It is this detachability that makes the assessment of Step 3 so essential to mimetic instruction and thus enables mimetic instruction to stratify students so effectively. Without a high likelihood that much of the knowledge that is presented will be forgotten, comparisons between students would be an ineffective way to measure student achievement.

A third characteristic of knowledge within the mimetic tradition is that "it can be judged right or wrong, accurate or inaccurate, correct or incorrect" (p. 118). These judgments are crucial for Step 3 of the method. If large numbers of students are to be evaluated efficiently, teachers need clear and certain standards.

Within the mimetic tradition, then, the teacher serves as the expert dispenser of knowledge—expert both because she possesses the knowledge that is to be presented and evaluated and because she is trained in the ways of presentation and evaluation. She knows the sum of 7 and 8, just as she knows the identity of Godzilla, and she knows how such knowledge is communicated to the student who does not know these things. In addition—and this is more important than it may appear at first—the teacher working within the mimetic tradition understands that it is her special role to transmit what she knows to her students—at least, some of what she knows. There is still the question of selecting the knowledge to be transmitted, but to explore this question, I want to turn to one of the most successful expositors and expositions of the mimetic tradition—E. D. Hirsch Jr. and the "core knowledge" of "cultural literacy."

CULTURAL LITERACY

In the book that introduced the term "cultural literacy," E. D. Hirsch Jr. argues that the transmission of information is the special function of public schools. He became aware of this simple truth, he says, as he began to recognize "the connection between specific background knowledge and mature literacy" (1987, p. 8). The ways in which "we apply past knowledge to the comprehension of speech" depend, Hirsch argues, on the application of prototypes (p. 51). Without these prototypes we are unable to understand written and oral language. The prototypes are representations of categories and may also be known as "frames, theories, concepts, models, and scripts" (p. 51). Hirsch, drawing on the work of R. C. Anderson, prefers the word *schema*, because "*Schema* and its plural *schemata* correctly suggest somewhat abstract mental entities rather than concrete images" (p. 51). Exactly what Hirsch has in mind by "mental entities"—how they are different from "concrete images" and why they are important—becomes clearer when he explains "the two essential functions" of schemata that make them "relevant to literacy. The first is storing knowledge in retrievable form; the second is organizing knowledge in more and more efficient ways, so that it can be applied rapidly and efficiently" (p. 56). In other words, schemata (as Hirsch understands them) have to do with knowledge, and with a particular notion of knowledge at that.

The concept of knowledge (and schemata) that Hirsch is working with coincides with the concept of knowledge within the mimetic tradition (as described by Jackson). Knowledge that is (in Hirsch's terms) storable and retrievable is clearly (in Jackson's mimetic terms) preexistent or secondhand and can therefore be transmitted from teacher or book to student.

Knowledge, as Hirsch conceives it, also fits the mimetic characterization of knowledge as something that can be judged "right or wrong, accurate or inaccurate, correct or incorrect." This notion (or kind) of knowledge does not fit everyone's understanding of schemata, but Hirsch thinks of schemata as "systems of relationships" describable in verbal formulations. Although he speaks of "two radically different types of schemata, one analogous to static pictures and another to scripts or procedures," it is really something more like definitions that Hirsch has in mind when he writes about schemata as "mental entities" (p. 56). His view of schemata emerged (as Hirsch explains in *Cultural Literacy*) when he discovered that some college students struggled with certain texts not because they lacked reading skill, but because they "lacked the background information needed for general literacy" (p. 47). One example that he gives of students' lack of background information comes from their attempts to read a paragraph describing Robert E. Lee's surrender to Ulysses S. Grant at Appomattox. "The community college test population," Hirsch says, "found this passage difficult to understand because they were, surprisingly, ignorant of the identities of Grant and Lee" (p. 41).

Hirsch explains that what these college students needed was not "profound knowledge," but rather "schematic information" such as:

1. America fought a Civil War.
2. The two sides were the Union and the Confederacy.

3. Grant was the chief general for the Union.
4. Lee was the chief general for the Confederacy.
5. The Union won. (p. 54)

This "schematic information" is precisely the sort of thing that can be judged "right or wrong, accurate or inaccurate, correct or incorrect." And if it sounds rather like definitions in a dictionary, that's not surprising. In "The Theory Behind the Dictionary: Cultural Literacy and Education," from the *New Dictionary of Cultural Literacy*, Hirsch explains that the idea of the dictionary came to him before he began to work on *Cultural Literacy*, which "was first conceived as merely a technical explanation of the ideas that led us to undertake the dictionary" (Hirsch, Kett, & Trefil, 2002, p. xii). From the beginning, Hirsch was primarily concerned not with the theory of cultural literacy, but with the systems of relationships, with the definitions, toward which the theory points. From the beginning, cultural literacy was for Hirsch a curricular idea, a project that was undertaken, he says, in the "hope it [would] help improve American public education and public discourse," presumably by providing a body of information that could be used by teachers and parents to instruct and assess children (p. xii). And one of the key features of this information is that it can be judged right or wrong.

As I match up Hirsch's notion of schemata (which he sees as knowledge storage systems) with Jackson's characterization of knowledge within the mimetic tradition, there is one significant point of difference: Jackson speaks of knowledge as forgettable, while Hirsch argues that cultural literacy is the knowledge that literate members of a society carry with them. The heart of the concept of "cultural literacy" is that there are pieces of knowledge that individuals do not forget: These facts have become part of the "collective memory" (Hirsch, Kett, & Trefil, 2002, p. xi). Hirsch is insisting that if individuals forget that "America fought a Civil War" or that "Grant was the chief general for the Union," they begin to lose their membership in American literate society. They begin, in fact, to cease to be Americans.

Hirsch's concern that information has been forgotten—or at least that it has been ignored in schools—fires his desire to reform schooling. Teachers, he fears, have been won over to "progressive" ideas and have neglected their responsibility to transmit the core knowledge of American culture. They have adopted a "content-neutral" approach to teaching that forgets to tell students the things they need to know if they are to be culturally literate. Hirsch sees this problem as fixable because all that is required to make children culturally literate is to teach them (that is, to present to them through the steps of the mimetic process) the information they need to know. By abandoning progressive, transformative, "content-neutral" curricula in favor of traditional, mimetic, fact-based curricula, schools will be able (Hirsch feels) to help all children become culturally literate. But what he has failed to realize is that it is traditional instruction—mimetic teaching—that is content neutral. That's the strength of mimetic instruction. The steps work for anything from tap dancing and typing to geometry and Greek literature. Hirsch embraced traditional instruction for its focus on the transmission of information, but he didn't seem to realize that dedicating ourselves to mimetically teaching "core knowledge" leaves open the question of what exactly that core knowledge is supposed to be. Mimetic instruction is a method of teaching, not a curriculum.

So how does Hirsch recognize what children need to know?

The answer to this question turns out to be rather surprising. Given Hirsch's aggressive critique of "content-neutral" teaching, one might suppose that the materials of instruction would be selected for their content—that is to say, for their intrinsic worth. But this is not the case. "Schematic information" (such as that needed by college students to read the paragraph about Grant and Lee) is not intrinsically valuable. The reason to know that "America fought a Civil War" is that this piece of information is valuable for understanding what other Americans say and write, not that possessing this information is inherently worthwhile, or that for its own sake it improves the quality of one's life. In another culture or at another time, knowing this information would likely be irrelevant and without value, and should not (from Hirsch's perspective) be taught. The *New Dictionary of Cultural Literacy* is not a source of wisdom but a collection of information that is deemed to be essential or fundamental only because it characterizes cultural literacy in 21st-century America. The fact that the book is a "new edition" makes the point: "A new edition is called for to keep up with the changes in American culture," changes that occur so quickly that *The New Dictionary of Cultural Literacy* is the third edition of the cultural-literacy dictionary to appear in less than 15 years (Hirsch, Kett, & Trefil, 2002, p. vii). This signifies more than just the financial success that Hirsch has achieved. "If a person or event has been widely recognized," write Hirsch and his fellow editors, "for more than fifteen years or seems likely to be recognized by a majority of people fifteen years from now, that person or event deserved consideration for a place in this dictionary" (p. xi).

But the editors could not wait 15 years to add 500 new items to the dictionary (p. vii). The content of the dictionary needed to be updated sooner, because the context of the dictionary had changed: America was a different place.

My point is that the information Hirsch identifies as essential is defined by what Stanley Fish would call an "interpretive community." These are groups

who share interpretive strategies not for reading but for writing texts, for con-
stituting their properties. In other words these strategies exist prior to the act
of reading and therefore determine the shape of what is read rather than, as is
usually assumed, the other way around (Fish, 1980, 14).

I am not suggesting that Fish and Hirsch would be able to agree about
the nature of the "interpretive strategies" employed by an "interpretive community." After all, when Fish introduced the idea of interpretive communities, he did so (in part) to explain how his idea of a "text" is different from
Hirsch's:

> The answer this book gives to its title question [Is there a text in this class?] is
> "there is and there isn't." There isn't a text in this or any other class if one
> means by text what E. D. Hirsch and others mean by it, "an entity which al-
> ways remains the same from one moment to the next" (Fish, 1980, p. vii).

But, Fish goes on, there is a text "if one means by text the structure of meanings that is obvious and inescapable from the perspective of whatever interpretive assumptions happen to be in force" (p. vii).

I am not going to try to spell out the interpretive assumptions or strategies that Fish has in mind. Suffice to say that he is not talking about some
key to literature in the form of a set of rules or guidelines suitable for reading any work anywhere at any time. Interpretive communities evolve and
their ways of making sense of language change. The point is that the content
of language is (in Fish's view) subordinate to the context of language (the
interpretive community). The meaning of a text (or better yet, the text itself)
depends on the situation, beliefs, problems, and ways of seeing the world of
those who make the meaning.

Limned with this broad stroke, Fish's belief in the existence of interpretive communities that structure the ways that language can make meaning
is not so different from Hirsch's belief in the existence of cultural literacy
that structures the ways that language can make meaning. The enormous
gulf between them only appears when Hirsch goes on to publish a dictionary intended to make manifest that structure, a task Fish would find non-
sensical, because the structure he is talking about cannot be reduced to
definitions.

For all their differences, though, Hirsch and Fish agree that the context
of telling—the situation and community in which language is written and
spoken—provides the only sure handle for grasping meaning. So how does
Hirsch recognize what children need to know? He looks at and listens to the
language of his world. Believing that information (definitions) make language
intelligible, Hirsch turns his hand to curriculum-making by selecting information (for its instrumental value) and organizing it into a dictionary and

graded schoolbooks. He asks, Is this information likely to be something that writers and speakers expect 21st-century Americans to possess? The information in turn guides the selection of materials for instruction. Readings are chosen because they contain the information found in the "collective memory"—a procedure and perspective most evident in Hirsch's series of schoolbooks, *What Your Kindergartner Needs to Know, What Your First Grader Needs to Know*, and so on.

The fourth-grade book, for example, is described as a "collection made for children" that "offers the academic core—the sort of core knowledge that the best educational systems provide to children all over the world" (Hirsch, 1992, p. xix). Like other books in the series, this book "builds upon knowledge presented in previous books," a point frequently restated (p. xix). Parents and teachers (the people to whom the book is addressed) are encouraged, for example, to have children refer to the maps from the earlier books in the series when reading the geography section of the fourth-grade book (p. 86). Later, parents and teachers are reminded that the study of Byzantium picks up the topic from the previous book ("a further look at Byzantium"). The concept of "knowledge" is also made explicit in this section: "One of the central tenets of *The Core Knowledge Series* is that knowledge builds on knowledge" (p. 114). Each piece of information leads to others, so that the books of the series (as well as the *New Dictionary of Cultural Literacy*) build a web of knowledge, or "systems of relationships."

From Hirsch's point of view, the building of this web of knowledge defines the context of classroom telling and offers what initially seems to be a plausible interpretation of the Godzilla story. A student who lacks key information is unable to perform a task. When she is provided with that information, she is able to move forward.

There are several problems with this reading, however. To begin with, the term *Godzilla* is not an element of "core knowledge": It does not appear in the *New Dictionary of Cultural Literacy*. Of course, that doesn't prevent a teacher from introducing the term (and the corresponding schematic information that identifies the term), but it raises an uncomfortable (for followers of Hirsch) possibility—namely, that the core of essential knowledge is not as clearly demarcated as teachers might hope. Cultural literacy may turn out to be far less definable than Hirsch supposes.

The other problems are even more serious. Hirsch's thesis ("knowledge builds on knowledge") posits a chain of connected bits of information. We might, for example, help a student to gain the knowledge that $7 + 8 = 15$ by introducing the information that $3 + 4 = 7$ or by defining the process of addition. But there is no path from the nature of Godzilla to $7 + 8 = 15$. That intellectual move cannot be an instance of knowledge building on knowledge, as Hirsch understands it.

The most serious problem in the mimetic/Hirsch reading of the Godzilla problem is the underlying assumption that the teacher's responsibility is to transmit to the student information she does not yet possess. To say that teaching the second grader about Godzilla leads her to see that 7 + 8 = 15 won't work, so how does she come to possess the arithmetic fact?

It seems more plausible that she possessed the fact all along, and that the problem was one of retrieval, but this doesn't overcome the inadequacy of any reading of the Godzilla story that the mimetic/Hirsch perspective can offer. By what organizational scheme would "Godzilla" be the trigger to recall "7 + 8 = 15"?

Advocates of the mimetic/Hirsch perspective might want to argue, at this point, that the Godzilla story is an educational oddity, a unique situation so far out of the norm of teaching that trying to explain it is at best a waste of time and probably misleading. If we found 1,000 other children puzzled by the same problem, would any of them be helped by some background on Godzilla? Perhaps not. And it's certainly true that if the story-problem context is removed, so that all that remains is "7 + 8 = ____," we would find that discussions of Godzilla helped no students whatsoever. My interaction with the second grader provides (it might be said) no insight or procedure that could ever be used by any other teacher with any other student.

From within the mimetic/Hirsch perspective, this indictment appears to me to be inescapable, but the case I am making in this book is that the ways students encounter teachers and telling are typically much more like the Godzilla story than the mimetic/Hirsch characterization of thinking and learning would allow. More immediately, I am arguing in this chapter that defining the classroom context of teachers-telling-students-things in terms of what students get out of a text (instead of what they do with a text) necessarily undermines thinking. To lend support to this assertion I'm going to turn now to a classroom study that shows how the mimetic/Hirsch notion of knowledge and knowledge-acquisition institutionalizes non-thinking.

TEACHING A NOVEL

In her paper "Testing, Tests, and Classroom Texts," Dorothea Anagnostopoulos looks at the ways in which an "external test" influenced how high-school teachers in four Chicago schools taught the Harper Lee novel *To Kill a Mockingbird*. The external test is the Chicago Academic Standards Exam (CASE), which "tested students' knowledge and mastery"of the core skills and content delineated in the Programs of Study (Anagnostopoulos, 2005, p. 35). While Chicago's Programs of Study and the exam are not explicitly derived from Hirsch's conception of core knowledge, the common elements are readily apparent. The Chicago Academic Standards Exam (for 10th graders) contains several questions, including a "constructed response" question, based on *To Kill a Mockingbird* and intended to assess students' knowledge of the basic facts of the work and of literary terms. Hirsch's schoolbooks and dictionary focus on the same kind of knowledge.

The effect of this sort of exam on the way that *To Kill a Mockingbird* was taught became apparent to Anagnostopoulos in the interviews she conducted:

> While the teachers mentioned several goals, including "exposing" students to a "classic," "realizing a historical perspective on the novel," and teaching students to "think and write critically," references to "covering" the "facts" of the novel to prepare students for the CASE permeated the interviews. Covering the novel meant focusing students' attention on identifying basic "facts," and, as Ms. Marshall, in Billings [High School], said, "just keeping track of the plot and details." (p. 49)

Ms. Marshall, says Anagnostopoulos,

> described the Program's suggested activities as "bogus," and noted that, because the district distributed sample test materials at the end of the semester, she was "going to copy the list (of literary terms) and they're going to look them up and memorize them. Another fine exercise in memorization courtesy of the Chicago Public Schools." (p. 50)

Hirsch, of course, would not be as dismissive as Ms. Marshall of the suggested activities. "Our current distaste for memorization," he says, "is more pious than realistic" (1987, p. 30). Confident that children need memorization to acquire the fundamental information of cultural literacy, Hirsch also believes that they revel in memorization. "At an early age when their memories are most retentive, children have an almost instinctive urge to learn specific tribal traditions. At that age they seem to be fascinated by catalogues of information" (1987, p. 30).

But despite this defense of memorization in *Cultural Literacy*, Hirsch's fourth-grade schoolbook emphasizes the need for children to find pleasure in poetry before they "study it technically." Their knowledge of poetry "should come first from pleasure and only later from analysis" (Hirsch, 1992, p. 42). Whether or not there is some sort of contradiction here is less important, however, than the assumption underlying Hirsch's argument—namely, that the aim of reading poetry is to acquire "knowledge of poetry." The students' acquisition of knowledge is precisely what Chicago's Programs of Study and the Academic Standards Exam are designed to accomplish. And these aims, Anagnostopoulos shows, become the aims of instruction. Although the teachers "stressed that they 'did not teach the test,' and that their previous experiences teaching the novel had a greater influence on their instructional decisions than did the district [curriculum guides]," Anagnostopoulos found that the teaching that went on was consistent with the aims of the Programs of Study and with the exam.

A striking example of the influence of test-based district guidelines on classroom teaching occurs when a discussion in Mr. Jones's and Ms. O'Reilly's co-taught class turns into a brief confrontation between two girls. One (White) girl asserts that a character (Mrs. Dubose) is right to refer to Atticus Finch (the father of the narrator and a White lawyer defending a Black man) as a "nigger lover." The other (Black) girl challenges this language, saying both that the assertion is wrong and that the White girl hasn't the right to use that language. After a brief back-and-forth exchange between the two girls, Mr. Jones steps in. "We don't have time to argue about stuff like this," he says, and he ends what he describes as a "childish argument." It's more important, he insists, for them to get back to the kind of information that will appear on the test. Anagnostopoulos summarizes the scene:

> Mr. Jones's reference to the CASE . . . relegated the girls' nascent attempts to talk about the issue of racism that lie at the novel's centre to "childish stuff," and situated it outside the boundaries of proper "academic" talk. According to Mr. Jones, the girls' exchange disrupted the real "academic" work of preparing for the test. (p. 58)

The discussion had begun when Ms. O'Reilly read a worksheet question asking why the narrator's brother (Jem) knocked down the flowers of Mrs. Dubose. When the first girl tried to attribute the act to Jem's attempt to get even with Mrs. Dubose for calling his father a "nigger lover," the discussion moved beyond the boundaries of the novel and toward a more general conversation about racism—a conversation the teacher felt obliged to shut down. The dampening effect of Mr. Jones's intervention on the discussion lingered for the remainder of the class. Later, when the question was posed again, the answer avoided the issue of racism: this time the student said simply, "Because Mrs. Dubose said that Atticus was no better than Tom Robinson [the Black defendant]." This response captured the facts of the novel and allowed the teaching and learning to focus on memorizing the information needed for the test. The context of the novel in this classroom (students get ready for an exam) overwhelmed the content of the novel.

As a result of such a redirection of a discussion, students discover that there is little need for them to think about a novel; what they need to do is to know it, be able to identify the characters and their actions. The institution of testing programs such as Chicago's Academic Standards Exam is, in effect, the institution of non-thinking. Within the context of such a testing program, stories (as Hirsch sees them) become repositories of information, vehicles of language that is to be mined for the facts it contains. An interpretive community (in this case, the authors of Chicago's Programs of Study, but in Hirsch's schools it would be the collective of the American culturally literate, as defined by Hirsch and his editorial team) determines the facts contained in examples of speech and writing. Students need not concern themselves with experiencing the content. They need only remember the pertinent facts, as defined by the interpretive community.

The fit between literature-as-information and testing programs is not, of course, limited to the city of Chicago or to teaching *To Kill a Mockingbird*. Robert Scholes, in *The Crafty Reader*, has discussed how English teachers around the country have shaped their teaching to fit tests:

> We [English teachers] were comfortable with tone, irony, paradox, and symbolism, and the makers of standardized tests were even more comfortable with them. Poetry, in the hands of the standardized testers, could serve as a vehicle to determine which students could find symbols, detect the presence of paradoxes, and perform other functions amenable to testing by multiple-choice questions and grading by machines (2001, p. 21).

I do not want to argue, however, that tests are somehow responsible for the institutionalization of non-thinking that occurs when the context of stories is equated with the process of acquiring information. Nor do I believe that it would be right to suppose that this perspective is forced on teachers by administrators or other actors outside the school. Anagnostopoulos's study reveals that teachers share and embrace this perspective in ways that go beyond the fit between instruction and standardized testing. The teachers, says Anagnostopoulos, "drew upon the norms and conventions that structure how literature is typically taught and read in secondary classrooms in the U.S." Even Ms. Marshall, who had described the district's suggested activities as "bogus,"

> did not oppose the conception of teaching and reading that the documents endorsed. When asked how she determined her objectives for tenth grade English, for example, Ms. Marshall noted the complementary relationship between the district's texts and her practices:
>
> > Ms. Marshall: For English 11? I think that's the objective of any English class. . . . They have to be familiar with aspects of plot, figurative language. They have to be able to write a persuasive essay and a narrative.

DA: Why?

MS. MARSHALL: We are told this by the Board.

DA: Would you do anything differently if the Board didn't tell you this?

MS. MARSHALL: No. (p. 50)

I am going to linger for a while over this "no." It is (at least to me) a surprising admission. A teacher who has openly expressed her scepticism about the educational benefit of having her students memorize the plot, characters, and language of a story now says she wouldn't do it any other way. This is, she says, "the objective of any English class." In part, she is speaking about the nature of subject matter and about what it is that defines English (or any other) class, a topic discussed in Part I. But I also believe that she is talking about the teacher-as-teller, that is, about the kind of telling that one is supposed to do if one is a teacher. This is the telling that Jackson refers to as "presenting" when he describes the stages of mimetic instruction—presenting skills and information. And though this kind of telling in the mimetic/ Hirsch mode seems especially likely to promote non-thinking, it turns out that looking at teaching this way has some advantages that may help to explain why Ms. Marshall and so many others wouldn't teach any other way. The teacher who presents texts (books, lectures, demonstrations, whatever) in a manner that focuses on the information that students are to get out of the texts is in an advantageous position to answer questions about fairness and significance in her teaching. She is well situated to argue that her teaching is equitable and that she is teaching students things that matter. These are important arguments for a profession more vulnerable than most to questions about its legitimacy, especially at a time when the institution most associated with the profession—public school—is frequently declared in public discourse to be failing. I'll be looking next at these two concerns— fairness and significance—before I return to the Godzilla story to reconsider what the second grader meant when she said, "I've got it." The aims (as they are embodied in the mimetic/Hirsch perspective) of squashing elitism and of making sure that teachers tell students things that matter will help me finally to get a better handle on what I believe the Godzilla story reveals about the influence of the context of telling on thinking and non-thinking.

MAKING CLASSROOM LIFE FAIR

The teacher who focuses on the information contained in texts, rather than on the experiences that students have in their encounters with the symbolic functioning of texts, avoids several problems. One of them is that while experiences cannot be programmed or guaranteed, information can. This means that it is easier to plan classes when the aim is for students to become "familiar with aspects of plot [and] figurative language" than it is to plan classes when the aim is for students to experience the symbolic functioning of, say, *To Kill a Mockingbird*. The two girls who argued about the epithet for Atticus Finch illustrated the difficulty a teacher can face. When students begin to talk about what a text means to them or how it makes them feel, the discussion may head off in directions the teacher did not prepare for, directions she may be unwilling to deal with.

A related, but even more daunting, problem for teachers that can be avoided by focusing on what students get out of texts (rather than on what they do with them) is assessment. Not only is it relatively easy to grade students on their mastery of information; it also seems to be marvelously equitable. Suppose, for example, that a teacher sees teaching *To Kill a Mockingbird* as an opportunity for her students to respond to the theme of racism. The two girls who argue about the epithet for Atticus Finch are beginning to seize the opportunity, but what about the rest of the class? What about students who read the book and get caught up in the drama of the trial and in the adventures of the Finch family, but do not see the racism as anything other than a character trait of a few misguided individuals? Can a teacher hold her students to account for what they cannot see?

The advantage of focusing on texts as tools for transmitting information is that the teacher can assume that all students (if they have not been placed in the wrong class) have the capacity to recognize the information. The teacher does not ask her students to see the social implications of a novel, the lyricism of a poem, the elegance of a geometry proof, the pathos of a symphony, or the mystery of a chemical reaction. She asks only that they see the information, and everyone can do that.

This perspective does not have to deny the existence of social implications, lyricism, elegance, pathos, and mystery. While Charles Dickens's infamous Mr. Gradgrind (from the novel *Hard Times*) pushes the perspective to that extreme, supposing that all such matters can be reduced to "fact" (if they exist at all), this portrait of the dry-as-dust pedant is too perfectly drawn. I suspect that all readers abhor what Gradgrind is, see through him, and deny that they are in any way like him. Because we are not like Gradgrind, we can congratulate ourselves on doing more than merely transmitting information. But what happens in our schools under the influence of the mimetic/Hirsch perspective is that social implications, lyricism, elegance, pathos, and mystery simply become new categories of secondhand information. This transmutation was chillingly portrayed by another 19th-century British writer, George Eliot, in her novel *Middlemarch*. She tells the story of young, high-minded Dorothea Brooke, who marries middle-aged scholar

Edward Casaubon. The two honeymoon in Italy, where Dorothea had expected that her erudite husband would instruct her, but the trip turns out rather differently from what she expected:

> [H]er husband's way of commenting on the strangely impressive objects around them had begun to affect her with a sort of mental shiver. . . .
>
> When he said, "Does this interest you, Dorothea? Shall we stay a little longer? I am ready to stay if you wish it,"—it seemed to her as if going and staying were alike dreary. Or, "Should you like to go to the Farnesina, Dorothea? It contains celebrated frescoes designed or painted by Raphael, which most persons think it worthwhile to visit."
>
> "But do you care about them?" was always Dorothea's question.
>
> "They are, I believe, highly esteemed."

And Casaubon then goes on to state what he understands to be the "the opinion of cognoscenti" (Eliot, 1872/1964, p. 194).

Casaubon knows a great deal about the sights in Italy. From the mimetic/Hirsch perspective of knowledge, he is knowledgeable. He does not esteem, but he knows what those who are learned profess to esteem. And he is, to Eliot his creator, a pitiable figure:

> It is an uneasy lot at best, to be what we call highly taught and yet not to enjoy: to be present at this great spectacle of life and never to be liberated from a small hungry shivering self—never to be fully possessed by the glory we behold, never to have our consciousness rapturously transformed into the vividness of a thought, the ardour of a passion, the energy of an action, but always to be scholarly and uninspired, ambitious and timid, scrupulous and dim-sighted (pp. 273–274).

While we teachers do not hope to be uninspired, timid, and dim sighted, or to include these aims in the mission statements of our schools, or to pass on these qualities to our students, the scholarliness of a Casaubon has its advantage. It removes any hint of elitism from learning and schooling because this sort of learning lies within reach of all students. When the inspirational message "all students can learn" is intoned, this is the sort of learning that is implied. All students can learn about the plot, characters, and themes in To Kill a Mockingbird or about the arrangements and colors in the paintings of Raphael or about a method of solving an algebraic equation. To ask for more—that students are moved to indignation because of a novel or to reflection because of a painting or to curiosity because of an equation—is to press for a kind of learning that all students cannot achieve. How can a teacher hold students to account for what they cannot see?

The teacher who defines what she tells students in terms of the context of the transmission of information avoids this conundrum. She asks the same of all students. She makes classroom life fair.

MAKING TEACHING MATTER

One of the banes of teachers' lives is to have a student challenge a classroom activity with the dreaded question, "Why do I have to learn this?"

Another way to put this question is, "Why are you telling me this?" and in this form the question is more easily recognizable as the essence of "context." In every instance of telling, the question "Why are you telling me this?" begs to be answered. The teacher who works within the transformative/progressive/child-centered tradition (in contrast with the mimetic/traditional/Hirsch tradition) has no answer to this question outside the story itself. If the student's encounter with, say, *To Kill a Mockingbird*, the history of the American Civil War, or a geometry proof fails to result in an experience that makes the telling matter, there is nothing outside the story to which the teacher can appeal to generate significance.

However, because the teacher working in the mimetic/Hirsch tradition defines *telling* in terms of the context of transmitting information, her answer to the question "Why are you telling me this?" is always implicitly present and separate from the story itself. Every instance of skillful teacher-telling (says Hirsch) reveals information, and the information is the "why." The information is what matters and what makes any instance of telling (think of Step 2 in the mimetic procedure) significant.

Of course, this answer holds little for students who are unconcerned with success in school, and it tends to corrupt even those who see school as a path to success. Emphasizing the telling and acquisition of information necessarily portrays education as preparation, a view that (as Dewey argued in *Democracy and Education*) leads to "a loss of impetus," "procrastination," and the "substitution of a conventional average standard of expectation and requirement for a standard which concerns the specific powers of the individual under instruction" (1916/1966, p. 55). It also leads, adds Dewey, to the institution of systems of punishments and rewards, a sure sign that students are guided in their action not by their engagement with the content of instruction, but rather by their response to the context of instruction. While most critics of schools are probably concerned with students who don't care about that context (the lack of "discipline" so often decried), some have recognized the corrupting influence of school life even on those who crave success. Denise Pope shows how the problems Dewey described almost a century earlier have come to life in high school students who excel at "doing school" (Pope, 2001). Having mastered the context of schooling, they find the content irrelevant. They succeed at being successful, but like Eliot's scholar Casaubon, they care about none of the learning they display.

The problem of student disengagement is not, however, a fatal critique for the mimetic/Hirsch perspective, because the claim Hirsch makes is that students need cultural literacy, not that they desire it or that it meets interests or that they care about it. They need it. They need it because, for Hirsch (and many others, of course), speaking facts is the only way to talk about the real world.

What I have in mind with this rather obscure expression—"speaking facts about the real world"—is a commonsense metaphysical stance. John Searle has expressed it this way:

> [T]here is a reality that exists totally independently of us, an observer-independent way that things are, and our statements about that reality are true or false depending on whether they accurately represent how things are. (1998, p. 134)

Hirsch has not, as far as I am aware, stated this view in so many words. The case he makes is, first, that information of some kind is necessary in order to make sense of language and, second, that the particular information he has collected in *The New Dictionary of Cultural Literacy* and in his schoolbooks is what's necessary to understand (and be understood in) the language of contemporary American society.

None of this requires that the "specific information" or "specific knowledge" teachers are supposed to present to students must accurately represent how things are, much less that there is an observer-independent reality, but I suspect that Hirsch simply takes that for granted. If the words that teachers say to students are going to matter, the words have to speak about something more than the use of language. When a student is told, for example, that "Central Powers" refers to "Germany and its allies (Austria-Hungary, Bulgaria, and the Ottoman Empire) in World War I," there is a tacit assumption that these words refer to real places and events in the real world (Hirsch, Kett, & Trefil, 2002, p. 221).

The assumption of observer-independent reality is not always so easy to recognize, however. Here is the entry for *Batman* from Hirsch's dictionary:

> A comic strip character that first appeared in 1939. With his faithful sidekick Robin (the Boy Wonder), Batman fights crime in Gotham City, foiling evil villains such as the Joker and the Riddler. (Hirsch, Kett, & Trefil, 2002, p. 30)

This "specific information" is a bit different from the entry for "Central Powers." Gotham City is not real in the sense that Bulgaria is real. The crimes that Batman and Robin fight are not real in the sense that World War I is real. Not even the time in which Batman's exploits occur is real. Robin was the Boy Wonder in 1939, and he was the same ageless boy in 2002 when the dictionary appeared. Neither Robin nor Batman ages, and the adventures of the two cannot be placed on the same time line with the dates of World War I (which can be found on page 247 of the dictionary in the "World War I" entry). This is not the observer-independent reality Searle was talking about.

But, of course, the key lies in the first line of the Batman entry: "A comic strip character that first appeared in 1939." Comic strips are real, and that "1939" is the same 1939 in which Germany invaded Poland to begin World War II. The rest of the entry describes the reality within the comic strip, which is to be read (as was *To Kill a Mockingbird* in the schools Anagnostopoulos observed) for the facts it contains. All realities are, from this metaphysical perspective, systems of facts nested within the facts of other realities. Through these systems of relationships, reality turns out to be observer-independent after all.

I am not sure that Hirsch has thought through or intends the assertions in the preceding two sentences. It may be a matter of indifference to which he has never given any thought, as his concerns are practical, and speculating about the nature of reality seems to have little to do with cultural literacy (except in the dictionary entry for "metaphysics"). It does seem to me, though, that the distinction between "observer-dependent" and "observer-independent" phenomena plays a crucial part in Hirsch's metaphysical perspective, because only the observer-independent can stand up as "specific knowledge." I doubt, that is, that Hirsch would agree when Searle says that "all functions are observer-relative" (1998, p. 121). What Searle has in mind is that when we impute teleology or motive to phenomena, we make a claim that depends on our own purposes and assumptions about the world. Others may suppose that the same structure or process performs an entirely different function. Searle's example is that asserting that the function of the heart is to pump blood follows "only because we take it for granted that life and survival are to be valued" (p. 122). Searle then goes on to contend that such observer-dependent phenomena become part of an external independent reality, that "the mind creates an objective social reality" (p. 111). Hirsch, however, concerned as he is with "specific information" and "specific knowledge," has no place for, or confidence in, observer-relative phenomena. In Hirsch's world, the function of the heart is as much an observer-independent phenomenon as its size or weight or the number of its valves.

Here is how the function of the heart is described in *What Your Fourth Grader Needs to Know*: "If your heart stopped beating, you would soon die. Why? The heart is responsible for keeping blood pumping throughout your body" (Hirsch, 1992, p. 329).

In some other book this use of the word *responsible* might be described as personification, a bit of metaphoric language intended to make the text more approachable and more interesting for 10-year-olds. But the epistemological premise of *What Your Fourth Grader Needs to Know*—"knowledge builds on knowledge"—obliges the reader to take seriously the statement that the heart "is responsible." The function of the heart is not (in Hirsch's world) observer-relative; it is a fact, a piece of specific information that children need to learn.

As long as teachers are speaking facts about the real world, they can be confident that they are telling students things that matter. What could matter more than facts about the real world? Besides, by restricting their telling to facts, they avoid awkward questions about the significance of their teaching. Unfortunately, they also create difficulties when they too narrowly limit what sorts of statements they can make about reality. They can be forced into accepting either dualism or materialism: Either mind and body are separate (so that connections between the two cannot be explained) or else one must deny that consciousness exists (see Searle, 1998, pp. 45–55).

In the classroom, speaking facts about the real world means that teachers all too often restrict themselves and their students (in their official business) to statements that have no subjective or experiential component. Students learn this metaphysical perspective early in their school careers. In one third-grade classroom I observed, when the class was studying the Navajo culture, the teacher asked the children if they would have liked to have lived in a Navajo village. No one would offer an answer until the teacher assured the children that it was all right for them to have an opinion. This skittishness about opinions remains a familiar feature of school life. I have often been asked by my students if it is all right, in a paper they are writing for class, to include their opinion. They have learned that, as Searle says, "Some of the features of the world exist entirely independently of us humans and of our attitudes and activities; others depend on us" (1998, p. 116); and they have learned that school is about those things that exist entirely independently of us. They have learned that opinions form a class of statements that are not ordinarily acceptable in the classroom, so that whatever thinking is associated with desiring, hoping, and valuing is out of place in school.

WORDS AND THE WORLD

Faced with the question, What do words do in the world? (which is another version of the question, Why do teachers tell students things?), the mimetic/Hirsch position responds, Words transmit information.

This is a tidy answer to a vexing problem. If telling students things is seen as the paradigm of teaching, some explanation has to be offered for what all that telling is supposed to accomplish. Some kind of case has to be made to explain the connection between words and the world, and this is a more difficult philosophical problem than the mimetic/Hirsch position acknowledges. Except in those instances when words are performatives ("Do you take this woman?" "I do"), words do not make things happen. The judge passes sentence, but the words do not incarcerate the prisoner; the jailer does.

And yet, we all know that words can hurt, and I suspect that when W. H. Auden (1958) wrote, "Poetry makes nothing happen," he was simply expressing a helplessness that many people felt in 1940, when the poem first appeared. He did, after all, spend his life writing poetry. In a different poem ("Words") Auden also wrote that a sentence "makes a world appear" (1960).

But even if we believe that somehow words do make things happen and words can even make a world appear, it remains a problem to explain how words do that, a problem nicely illustrated in Robert Coles's book *The Call of Stories*. A little more than halfway through this book, Coles takes up the question of how it is that stories shape the "moral imagination." He writes about a class of his that was discussing a story by Flannery O'Connor. "How does a story change people?" a student wants to know. How does a story "take the wind out of a big shot" as some of the students in class had claimed? As Coles puts it, "The student wanted a specific exposition of what literature offers the moral life, meaning our moral understanding of things, and meaning above all, our moral conduct." How, that is to say, can words make things happen?

In the context of a class spent exploring the moral significance of stories, the question must have sounded like the comment of a cheeky student trying to point out a teacher's embarrassing oversight. In fact, Coles feels obliged to assure the reader that the question "was not meant to be ironic." But he also has to acknowledge the absence of an answer: "None of us was able to produce, on the spot, a confident statement of cause and effect." The class made a stab at an answer, however. They "pointed out to one another that a story is not an idea" and that "reading a story is not like memorizing facts." They spoke of "memories," "feelings," "responsiveness," "heightened awareness," and "felt experience." Coles concludes that while a novel sometimes can be

> polemical argument . . . it can, as well, insinuate itself into a remembering, daydreaming, wondering life; can prompt laughter or tears; can inspire moments of amused reflection with respect to one's nature, accomplishments, flaws. (1989, pp. 126–128)

Coles doesn't tell us if this line of thinking satisfied the student who wanted to know how it is that stories change the world. The case Coles makes asserts that reading stories promotes emotional reactions, but does this answer the student's question? It might, but whether it does depends on one's answer to that old metaphysical question: What is the nature of reality? Does our experience (remembering, daydreaming, wondering) structure or even create the world? If so, Coles has answered the student's question.

But he's missed the point if the student is one of those who suppose that remembering, daydreaming, and "moments of amused reflection" are experiences that go on inside a person's head, not events that happen outside, in the world. If one supposes that reality is made up of objective facts, not subjective experience, talking about how a story makes one feel doesn't say anything about the real world. Words may cause people to laugh or cry, but words still don't move the furniture, buy the groceries, or mow the lawn.

If E. D. Hirsch Jr. had been sitting in on the conversation in Coles's classroom, he probably would have stepped in when the students began talking about how a story is "not like memorizing facts." Certainly, he might have said, reading a story is not the same as memorizing the state capitals, but to understand a story one has to get the facts, which means knowing and remembering whom the story is about and what happens in it. Also (he might have continued), understanding a story means seeing how it is a template for our lives, a sort of big fact by which we measure our actions. When we read about young George Washington telling his father the truth about chopping down the cherry tree (Hirsch would say, noting that the tale is included in his schoolbook series), we learn what it means to be truthful and how to be truthful in our own lives. Stories, like every other use of words (he would conclude), convey information, and that's how they change people and how they make things happen.

The issue, it seems to me, is how we understand the nature of reality. Does our experience structure the world in which we live or is it an incidental outcome of the workings of external facts? Are social implications, lyricism, elegance, pathos, and mystery aspects of life that can be studied directly or must they be mediated through authorities and learned as external facts? Can our teaching deal with observer-relative phenomena? These are not questions that many teachers consciously ponder, but if Philip Jackson is right to say that the history of teaching can be understood in terms of the yin and yang of mimetic and transformative traditions, teachers are weighing in on the nature of reality whether or not they intend to. Hirsch and Cunningham are weighing in on the question too, and it is because that metaphysical question lies at the heart of these debates about the context of schooling that Hirsch and Cunningham feel such urgency and that Cunningham insists that no compromise is possible between traditional and progressive teaching. To accommodate the two traditions of teaching that are, according to Cunningham, doing "battle" would require a philosophical journey that

Cunningham is unprepared to make. He would be letting go of that reality that exists totally independently of experience.

GODZILLA'S RETURN

But how does this talk of metaphysical questions bear on the Godzilla story and on the second grader whose face lit up knowingly when she said, "I've got it," and went to her seat and answered the arithmetic problem? My answer is that I have been facing a metaphysical question ever since I asked, What is it that she "got"?

The second grader's problem was not that she couldn't fill in the blank in this number sentence: "7 + 8 = ____." She remembered that and other basic arithmetic facts. She understood the concept of addition, so that if she were shown a picture of 7 houses next to a picture of 8 houses and asked how many houses there would be if they were all on the same street, she would have come up with the answer "15." Her difficulty lay in knowing when to use this knowledge and skill. In what situations was she supposed to draw on this particular ability? When she said, "I've got it," what she meant (it seems to me) was that she had figured out which game she was supposed to be playing, and she knew what knowledge she needed to draw upon to play this game. When she said, "I've got it," she was talking, not about the number 15, but about the context in which she, the word problem, her teacher, and an imaginary monster could all coexist.

All of us have found ourselves in similar situations, in which we have been stymied, only to suddenly realize with chagrin, "I knew that!" What comes to us in a flash is how one piece of information or one way of seeing gives meaning to what was confusion only a moment before. It is because of the infrequency of this phenomenon that teachers so often complain that students fail to demonstrate what they have been taught. The problem is that, while rules of arithmetic (or names, dates, or terminology) can be given to students, there are no rules for when to apply this knowledge; there can be no algorithm for determining the "specific knowledge" that is called for in a particular context. The use of information is a response that requires thinking and creativity. If a teacher attempts to tell students which information or fact or procedure a situation calls for, she simply turns the application of the information into another piece of information, and once again the student is faced with the question of when to apply it.

When the second grader asked me for help with the Godzilla story problem, I could have told her, "You're supposed to add these two numbers—7 and 8." I could also have told her that when she sees story problems that contain the words *all together*, she is probably supposed to add some (or all) of the numbers in the problem. But even if she remembers this rule of thumb, the advice won't tell her for certain whether she is supposed to add together some numbers the next time she sees the words *all together*. We can be definitive about the "specific knowledge" that students are supposed to get out of curricula (the things we tell them), but we cannot be equally definitive about when and how they should use the things we tell them without turning the use itself into another piece of knowledge without a context.

A high-school English teacher could tell her students that *To Kill a Mockingbird* is a book about racism. She could point out elements of their own community that reflect the issues suggested by the book. She would, in effect, be telling them that what they have been told about their community should be seen as parallel to what they have been told about the book. This may prepare students for test questions over *To Kill a Mockingbird*, but does it help them to read, say, Martin Luther King Jr.'s letter from the Birmingham jail? Not necessarily. There is no teacherly help that will guarantee that someone will see a connection in a new situation. We can tell a student that a connection exists, but we cannot teach a student a procedure that will guarantee that the student will recognize a connection between what was seen yesterday and what is seen today for the first time.

Teachers can try to make classroom life fair by holding students accountable only for what the teacher can tell, but the result is that non-thinking is encouraged, or even required.

Teachers can try to make the content of their teaching significant by adhering to a kind of naive realism according to which students are accountable only for that which is objectively true, but again this undermines thinking because it reduces learning to the pedantic accomplishments of a Casaubon.

Knowing that in this situation, this context, I should add these two numbers is a separate matter from knowing what the two numbers add up to. And it is a kind of knowing that cannot be told to a student; it is a response to telling, not the content of telling. A teacher's attempts to make classroom life fair and to tell students things that matter tend to make it unnecessary for students to respond. All they have to do is to reproduce what the teacher told them.

PART III

The Paradox of Believing

CHAPTER 5

The Whole Truth

S tudents believe things.

In part this believing reflects their nature as students: If they are really to be students (something more than sitting in a classroom), they need to believe, for example, that their teachers are trying to tell the truth, that what they study is worthwhile, that they are capable of learning.

But most of a student's believing is not a matter of student nature; it is a matter of human nature. If we "take a view of the Opinions of Mankind," says John Locke,

> observe their Opposition, and at the same time, consider the Fondness, and Devotion wherewith they are embrac'd; the Resolution, and Eagerness, wherewith they are maintain'd, [we] may perhaps have Reason to suspect, That either there is no such thing as Truth at all; or that Mankind hath no sufficient Means to attain a certain Knowledge of it. (1700/1975, p. 44)

Human beings (Locke is saying) do not just entertain opinions. We eagerly resolve ourselves to propagate them, we revel in them, we devote our lives to them, and we defend them against the challenges of other people with other opinions even when we cannot defend the claims our opinions entail. Our ability to embrace opinions—to believe—runs far ahead of our ability to "attain a certain Knowledge."

Some of these "beliefs" that we embrace and maintain concern the grand abstractions—democracy, justice, the search for truth, God. These are the sorts of things we say we believe in, and saying that, we acknowledge them as stances or relationships, as means of placing ourselves within the social and natural worlds. They are the nonproblematic (and therefore invisible) elements of our environments through which we see and think about those elements that task, perplex, trouble, and torment us. When we say that we believe in something, we are saying that this something is where we take our stand in order to think about other matters.

Most of our beliefs are not so lofty as those concerning God and justice. We may believe in dental hygiene and exercise as promoters of health, in either phonetics instruction or whole-language instruction as the true promoter of literacy, in the reduction of taxes as a policy for increasing revenue, in astrology as a predictor of human events, or in the wisdom of one political candidate rather than another as the best hope for the welfare of the nation. With these beliefs too, when we say we believe in them, we are saying this is where we take our stand in order to think about such matters as buying toothpaste, joining the YMCA, selecting instructional materials for a class of first graders, endorsing or opposing a bill in Congress, choosing a mate, or voting in the next election.

As I said in Chapter 1, Dewey treats beliefs as the most restricted sense of the terms *thinking* and *thought*, and he divides beliefs into two categories according to whether there is an "attempt to state the grounds that support" the belief and whether the basis for the belief is adequate. But there is, of course, a difficulty with this distinction between beliefs that rightfully command our respect and those that do not. A belief is not a hunch or hypothesis. The holder of a belief always feels that the basis for the belief is adequate: This is what believing means. Plato saw this as perhaps the fundamental educational problem. In the dialogue *Sophist*, the Visitor (taking the role usually occupied by Socrates) states the problem this way:

> VISITOR: I think I see a large, difficult type of ignorance marked off from the others and overshadowing all of them.
> THEAETETUS: What's it like?
> VISITOR: Not knowing, but thinking that you know. That's what probably causes all the mistakes we make when we think. (229c; all quotes from Plato, 1961)

Here is the third paradox of thinking in classrooms: When students think, they begin their work with what they know—that is, what they believe. Thinking cannot begin from a void; we are always in the middle of our lives, and the thinking that we do is in part constituted of beliefs about our self and about the worlds in which we live. But believing is the end of thinking; it is the satisfaction of intellectual closure. It is, in the language of Bertrand Russell, a sort of "rest and peace" that approaches "ecstasy," but it is no longer thinking (1939/1967). When we are thinking, we are also believing, but believing is the end of thinking. In the final two chapters I deal with this paradox of believing. In the following chapter, I will look at how thinking for oneself is possible. In this chapter I turn to the ways in which the problem of truth has been understood in schools and to how this understanding has shaped thinking and encouraged non-thinking.

YEARNING FOR MEANING

Denise Pope (2001), in *"Doing School": How We Are Creating a Generation of Stressed Out, Materialistic, and Miseducated Students*, looks at the lives of a group of "successful" high-school students and discovers that doing well in school is not the same as finding the content of schooling meaningful and important. Students can seemingly master schooling without caring about learning. Pope concludes that the pressure to succeed at "doing school" overwhelms interest in the intrinsic benefits of schooling. Robert Fried (1996) describes the problem as it concerns all students and teachers and calls it the "game of school."

These portraits of school might be taken as evidence of apathy and disengagement from any desire for meaningfulness, but it seems to me that the opposite is closer to what is happening. The disengagement described by Pope testifies to the yearning for meaning felt by the students she observed, the yearning for meaning felt by all humans. What has happened to these students, in part, is that their instinctive yearning for meaning—the sort of thing I suspect Aristotle had in mind when he wrote, "All men by nature desire to know"—is out of place in an institution that recognizes only a desire for truth (980a22; all quotes from Aristotle, 1984).

I can illustrate the difference I have in mind between "meaning" and "truth" with an episode from one of the undergraduate courses I teach. I told the students a story about a fifth-grade classroom I had observed. The teacher in my story was conducting a lesson on the topic of "working for peace in the world." He had begun by asking the fifth graders if they remembered some of the ways in which one could work for peace, topics discussed in previous lessons. These included banning nuclear weapons, engaging in nonviolent protests, and boycotting in order to advance civil rights. As he reviewed this material, a girl sitting directly in front of where the teacher was standing turned to the boy next to her and yelled out, "You stepped on my foot!"

The boy protested just as loudly that he'd done no such thing. The girl repeated her charge, and the boy denied it. This continued until the teacher stepped between them and told them to be quiet and to move their desks farther away from each other's. He complained that their behavior was unacceptable and that it was just this sort of digression that all too often interfered with worthwhile discussions in his classroom.

"Now," he said, "let's get back to talking about how we can work for peace in the world."

That was the story I told my undergraduate class in my Foundations of Education course, and at the end of the story, one of my students raised her hand and said, "He missed a teachable moment."

This comment—"He missed a teachable moment"—effectively ended discussion of the story. Nothing more needed to be said, because the episode had been named, and the naming showed what education students should learn from the episode. The lesson was complete.

At the time I was not alert enough to recognize what had happened. I had offered a story as part of the ongoing aim of the course to explore the meaning of classroom life, and I had been presented with a truth. What I had seen as a situation fraught with ambiguity was for my student a matter of fact. Her instinct to state the fact is understandable. In school life the yearning for meaning is routinely transformed into a desire for truth, which is to say, a desire to reduce experience to a matter of truth. Unfortunately, we lose much in this transformation; as Dewey wrote, "meaning is wider in scope as well as more precious in value than is truth" (quoted in Kestenbaum, 2002, p. 2). Hannah Arendt even argues that the move from meaning to truth obviates the need for thinking. "The need of reason"—or thinking—"is not inspired by the quest for truth but by the quest for meaning" (quoted in Kestenbaum, 2002, p. 89). Besides experiencing the loss that accompanies the narrowing of focus from meaning to truth, we also (when we make this move) unwittingly enmesh ourselves in a labyrinth of unresolved problems. In this chapter I want to sketch the nature of some of these problems. I want to show how the problem of truth warps classroom life and encourages non-thinking. I begin with one of the most common of the "thinking skills" activities in schools, an activity that unambiguously expresses the desire for truth.

FACTS AND OPINIONS

Beginning in their years of elementary school and continuing through college, U.S. students are often instructed in (and assessed at) telling the difference between a fact and an opinion. Quizzes over this topic often look like the one below that I gave to a group of graduate students, who were themselves teachers.

FACT OR OPINION?

Write *F* or *O* to indicate if the statement is properly classified as a fact (F) or an opinion (O).

_____ 1. There are nine students in this class.
_____ 2. Amy is the tallest student.

_____ 3. Jessica is the smartest student.

_____ 4. Patrick is the most attractive student.

_____ 5. George Washington was born on February 11, 1731.

_____ 6. One of the major causes of the American Civil War was the inability to resolve the problem of slavery.

_____ 7. On average over the last 100 years in New Orleans, rain has fallen on 23 days in July each year.

_____ 8. On most afternoons in July in New Orleans, it rains.

_____ 9. It will probably rain on Thursday in New Orleans.

_____ 10. A 2003 Jaguar XJ8 costs $96,000.

_____ 11. I paid $92,583.49 for my 2003 Jaguar XJ8.

_____ 12. A 2003 Jaguar XJ8 costs too much.

_____ 13. A 2003 Jaguar XJ8 costs too much for most people to be able to buy one.

_____ 14. This quiz made no sense to most of the students who have taken it.

_____ 15. This quiz makes no sense.

For the most part, my students agreed about their answers to these items. They unanimously agreed, for instance, that items 1 and 2 are facts and that items 3 and 15 are opinions. And they agreed as well about what it is that makes 3 and 15 different from 1 and 2: Counting and measuring height are well-established procedures about which everyone agrees, but "being smart" and "making sense" are concepts that are too slippery to allow for agreement about either what they refer to or how to measure them.

I suspect that most people who have been schooled in the differences between facts and opinions would respond similarly, but there is nevertheless something odd about this way of looking at the world. Because they are teachers, my students make decisions every day about the quality of their own students' schoolwork. They decide which students are doing "A" work and which ones are not passing the course at all. They decide which questions are answered correctly, which problems are solved logically, which essays are written clearly and informatively. Some of them may be asked to write letters of reference to help others decide which students most deserve to be admitted to a prestigious university. In short, it is the business of my students (as it is of other teachers) routinely to make judgments about whether their students are "being smart" and "making sense."

In fact, it is their business to teach their students to recognize "being smart" and "making sense." "Thinking skills" activities (like lessons about distinguishing facts from opinions) are supposed to help us be smarter and make better sense. The lessons would not exist if we did not believe these goals to be possible. Our school policies of assessment, grouping, promotion, and selection show that we believe that "being smart" and "making sense" are qualities or characteristics that can be striven for and practiced by students, as well as being taught, measured, and rewarded by teachers. So when a group of teachers says that "being smart" and "making sense" are merely matters of opinion, they bring into question the work that they do and the judgments they make. They undermine their own expertise.

Why do they do this?

The answer, it seems to me, has to do with the beliefs that they bring to epistemology (which is, after all, the field of study in which fact-and-opinion exercises belong). They believe that there are many ways of being smart and that all these ways deserve to be encouraged. They believe that things that make sense to one person don't necessarily make sense to another and that this difference in capacity to comprehend does not equate with difference in merit. They believe that picking out one person from a group as "smarter" than the others is somehow unkind to those others, and unkind in a way that constitutes behavior that teachers ought not to exhibit. There are probably other beliefs involved in the claim that "being smart" and "making sense" are slippery concepts, but these examples suffice to show why my students concluded that items 3 and 15 of the quiz are statements of opinion. For each of these beliefs includes with it the overarching belief that says that a statement is either a fact or an opinion, and if judgment is involved, it is an opinion.

We might attempt to save this situation by arguing that teachers' opinions about such matters as "being smart" and "making sense" are better founded and more worthy than the opinions of those who are not teachers. This attempt fails, however. In the first place, as demonstrated by our current national mania for accountability through testing, we (as a society) do not believe that teachers' opinions about these matters are well founded and persuasive. We want "science-based" numbers; we want facts. Second, the commonly held distinction between facts and opinions undercuts any argument that one opinion is more tenable than another. If an opinion is a statement that is "not fact," what can be offered as a basis for arguing the superiority of one opinion over another?

The effect of this logical dead end on students was observed and lamented by Katherine Simon in her book *Moral Questions in the Classroom*. Too often, she says, classroom discussions that she observed were empty because of this division between fact and opinion:

> It is as though the spheres of "fact" and "opinion" have been given restraining orders, forbidding them from mingling with each other. When the floor is open for opinion, . . . research data have no place; when, on the other hand, there are facts to cover, moral and existential questions—full of controversy, complexity, and ambiguity—are banished. (Simon, 2001, p. 94)

In a world in which fact and opinion cannot interpenetrate each other, thinking is constantly thwarted. Facts lead nowhere, and opinions stand on nothing. Beliefs exist and cannot be questioned. How have we arrived at this educational dead end, and how can we avoid it? How can students both believe and think? To suggest an answer to these questions I want to look more closely at a bit of the philosophical debate that underlies common notions of fact and opinion.

THE PROBLEM OF TRUTH

Questions about the nature (or even the possibility) of "truth" plagued 20th-century thought and have been embedded in schooling, especially in the ways in which we teach and talk about fact and opinion. Speaking in 1897 about "the problem of knowledge," John Dewey said prophetically, "Strange as it may sound, the question which was formulated by Kant [How is knowledge possible?] is the fundamental political problem of modern life" (1897/1977, p. 61).

The possibility of knowledge became a political problem, Dewey says, because of the emergence of the "conception of progress" and of the "conception of the individual as the source and standard of rights" (p. 61). Truth (Dewey says) can no longer be considered to be merely received; because of what has been achieved technologically and socially, we recognize that truths must be created and re-created from the problems encountered within the life of a progressive society. Just as the experiments of scientists rewrite the sciences, so too the experiments of a progressive society rewrite our social and moral understanding, as, for example, when the concept of a citizen is redefined by establishing a woman's right to vote.

But if knowledge is constructed through debate over how a progressive society interprets and defines individual rights, how can the authority of truth be secured? The method Dewey recommends is science—that is, experience—a method that provides a procedure but leaves truth in a constant state of emergence. So, he says, "The possibility of getting at and utilizing this truth becomes therefore the underlying and conditioning problem of modern life" (p. 61).

A little more than a decade later, in a series of lectures on "the problem of truth," Dewey expanded on this theme of emerging truths, beginning with the observation that "when Truth is, so to say, individualized, when it is spoken of as an integer, dominant political, moral, and religious beliefs are indicated." People do not put the capital *T* on *Truth* unless they want to add some obligation of conduct to an assertion, "a general view of things upon which one should regulate one's affairs" (Dewey, 1911/1998d, p. 102). This means, among other consequences, that the defined Truth is fixed and has lost its intellectual quality. "[N]o genuinely intellectual proposition," he says, "implies an assertion of its own truth" (p. 117). Intellectual propositions (unlike beliefs or Truth) are problematic, doubtful situations. In contrast, "Truth as a positive, achieved thing simply means that use *has* tested and *has* approved what was an intellectual, and so problematic affair, and thereby has given it an assured status in further effort" (p. 118). Truths are thus bound up in doing, and this reconception of truth as a tentative result of experience to be tested by further experience seems to Dewey to be a philosophical position that demands assent. The "identification of truth . . . with working towards the concrete production of specific consequences" is, he says, an "impregnable stone wall" that neither realist nor idealist can butt through. This way of looking at truth does, however, point toward "the debatable ground in the evolution of a pragmatic philosophy." Can "intellectually objective" and "socially controlling" truths converge? (p. 123) Can we create a society in which emerging small-*t* truths are employed with the socially controlling force of capital-*T* Truth?

Dewey says yes, arguing that "the standpoint and method of science [which offer intellectually objective truths] do not mean the abandonment of social purpose and welfare as rightfully governing criteria in the formation of beliefs [socially controlling Truth]" (p. 123). He looks to the day when science will discover new social purposes and rewrite social welfare. And so he concludes "that objective truth means interpretations of things that make these things effectively function in liberation of human purpose and efficiency of human effort" (p. 128). Only truth that is "operative in human affairs" (p. 122) can be of use to (or true for) human beings.

A little more than 25 years later Dewey took up these issues in his book *Logic: The Theory of Inquiry*. Here he does not use the word *truth*, and he warns readers about the ambiguity of the word *knowledge*. "That which satisfactorily terminates inquiry," he says, "is by definition, knowledge" (1938/1998c, p. 161). Too often, he continues, people conclude that this observation is "something significant," instead of what it really is—a tautology. Inquiry is not to be defined in terms of knowledge or of truth, as if what is known can precede what is found out. Knowledge or truth is defined in terms of inquiry. In fact, one of the results of inquiry is the discovery of what constitutes appropriate method, so that logical thinking is itself an outcome of inquiry.

Instead of beginning with given, fixed material, inquiry begins with what Dewey calls "an indeterminate situation." He says, "Inquiry is the directed or controlled transformation of an indeterminate situation into a determinately unified one" (1938/1998b, p. 178). The "situation" is for Dewey an "interaction" between the knower and the known, although a sharp demarcation of knower and known is far from what Dewey intends. "Nature," he says, "is an environment only as it is involved in interaction with an organism, or self, or whatever name be used" (p. 172). Inquiry changes the environment as surely as it changes the inquirer.

Because "inquiry is a *continuing* process" (Dewey, 1938/1998c, p. 161), Dewey prefers not to speak of knowledge or truth, but rather of "warranted assertibility" (p. 160). Forty years after he predicted that the problem of knowledge would be the "fundamental problem of modern life," he finds that even the words *knowledge* and *truth* are best avoided. But it may be that he avoids them not because of a conceptual difficulty, but because, for Dewey, there really is no problem of truth or problem of knowledge. "Truth" and "knowledge," for Dewey, have been irrevocably transformed through the triumph of the inquiry that is experience. The problem of truth or knowledge is a problem that occurs for those who refuse to accept this transformation.

One of those refusers was Bertrand Russell. Responding to Dewey's book *Logic: A Theory of Inquiry*, Russell challenged Dewey's attempt to base logic upon inquiry rather than upon truth. He says:

> Knowledge, if Dr. Dewey is right, cannot be any part of the ends of life; it is merely a means to other satisfactions. This view, to those who have been much engaged in the pursuit of knowledge, is distasteful. (Russell, 1939/1967, p. 205).

Russell's objection goes deeper than a desire to defend the pursuit of knowledge as one of life's noble ends. He worries, too, that without "truth," to speak of "the ends of life" is meaningless gibbering. "We act," he says,

> in so far as we are not blindly driven by instinct, in order to achieve ends which are not merely further actions, but have in them some element, however precarious and however transient, of rest and peace—not the rest and peace of mere quiescence, but that kind that, in the most intense form, becomes ecstasy. (p. 205)

Without ends beyond inquiry, life becomes the proverbial rat race. We chase and are chased; we buy and sell; we get and spend; we "lay waste our powers"; and we find no peace.

Russell's objection to basing logic upon inquiry rather than upon truth goes deeper even than the futility of this endless circle of inquiring. He feels in Dewey's position an empty ache, an inability to receive the world fully. "Activity," says Russell, "can supply only one half of wisdom; the other half depends upon a receptive passivity" (p. 205). To be wise, to possess the knowledge that passes understanding, requires receptivity, it requires openness. And what is it that Russell would be open to? It is the Truth—capital *T*—that is in the world. Dewey's conception of inquiry as a transaction, an interaction with the environment, strikes Russell as impossible and absurd. Astronomers, he says, do not change the stars by observing them. Truths about the stars are not transacted; they are discovered by those who are open to them.

Now, this all-too-brief look at a portion of the lifelong debate between Dewey and Russell is not intended to stand as the whole story of the problem of truth, which includes many other players and many other questions (consider Husserl, Heidegger, Wittgenstein, Ryle, Popper, Sartre, Arendt, Quine, and Gadamer, for example), but it illustrates some of what is at issue when I claim that the problem of truth plagued 20th-century thought. The great cultural debates of the 20th century—about the uses of technologies for everything from making life to making war, the expansion of civil rights, women's movements, the separation of church and state, the limitation of rights by the state in the name of security, the definitions of family and marriage—all are affected by the problem of truth. Our cultures, our ways of life, and our beliefs about education are shaped both by Dewey's vision of the construction of knowledge and by Russell's hunger for Truth.

It is arguable that we are only now, a little more than 100 years after Dewey announced the problem of truth to be the "fundamental political problem of modern life," realizing the terrible reality of his prophecy. The revitalization of fundamentalist movements around the world and the violence those movements have sometimes inspired represent an inevitable response to the problem of truth.

At any rate, it is obvious, I suppose, that this problem is crucial to schooling. One of the substructural assumptions of teaching is truthfulness: Teachers are supposed to tell students the truth (Jackson, Boostrom, & Hansen, 1993, pp. 16–24). Textbooks are supposed to embody and convey knowledge. Decisions about what goes into the curriculum hang upon how we conceive of truth and upon what we believe is true. Debates rage about curriculum and textbooks and the methods of measuring exactly what it is that students are supposed to learn, and they rage so fiercely precisely because Truth eludes us, precisely because "Human beings can at present only ascertain that a judgment *so far* coheres with their system of harmonious judgments" (Shook, 2000, p. 130).

And the problem of truth cuts even closer than this to the heart of teaching and learning, for it is part of the legacy that children bring with them when they come to school. Like all of us, they yearn for meaning, for something that matters in their lives. But when this yearning is reduced to a desire for truth, they are stuck (whether or not they recognize or are able to articulate it) with the question "How does thought hook onto the world?" (Jolley, in Irwin, Conrad, & Skoble, 2001, p. 281). How can the desire for truth become a means of comprehending reality?

The problem of truth is not that the answers to life's questions elude us, but that when we insist on answers to questions, when we suppose that "truth" is the same as "meaning" and that the problem of truth may be all right for philosophers to worry about but has nothing to do with schools, we make it impossible for us or our children to think about the things we care about the most. Because that statement may seem too strong, I want to support it by looking at how a particular curriculum question is warped by the problem of truth.

CREATION SCIENCE

In my community (as in many others in the United States) there have been periodic efforts to encourage the school board to mandate the teaching of "creation science" as an alternative for certain aspects of geology, astronomy, and biology. If I am asked by the local newspaper or television station to respond (in my capacity as a member of the educational establishment) to the request that creation science be added to the school curriculum, what should I say? Part of me says that everything should be studied. I am someone who believes in the free exchange of ideas, someone who believes that when issues are discussed openly, truth will prevail.

And I know that the assumption of truthfulness does not mean that untruths never exist in school curricula. Untruths are commonplace. Often they are openly presented as untruths, as beliefs embraced before people became enlightened. Ninth-grade English teachers across the United States teach Greek mythology without anyone supposing that this promotes animism or polytheism.

Other untruths are presented, not as mistakes from long ago, but in the guise of truth. When I was in elementary school, I learned that all matter is composed of atoms, which are in turn composed of protons, electrons, and neutrons—which were supposed to be the ultimately small particles. This was at a time when particle physicists were already exploring neutrinos and quarks, although it was admittedly before superstring theory emerged. Also when I was in elementary school, I was taught that Columbus was a great hero, a man of insight who maintained his faith in a spherical Earth, even when those around him thought him crazy for it. Now, of course, Columbus is more of a villain, an embodiment of oppressive colonialism, and we know that belief in a spherical Earth was common in his time and that his plans for a westward voyage were opposed because the ships of the time were not thought to be sturdy or large enough to sail west to the shores of China. Most of the experts thought the earth was quite a bit larger than Columbus thought it was, and they were right.

So I know that curricula often contain untruths, and experience shows (I believe) that over time, truths (with Dewey's small *t*) prevail. I believe in the free exchange of ideas. At least, I claim to believe in that. But I also fear that creation science undercuts astrophysics, geology, biology, and even the premises that make possible the very concept of science.

I am not comforted by those who say that teaching *about* creation science is no different from teaching *about* Norse mythology, the lost continent of Atlantis, or phrenology. In order for this position to be reassuring, it is necessary to maintain that all instruction is teaching *about*. If one supposes that children perceive multiplication facts, the major battles of World War I, and the conjugation of the verb *avoir* as assertions that require interpretation and evaluation, then adding creation science to the list of topics that students ponder poses no reason for concern. But the things that students are supposed to know in school are not typically presented to them as claims, assertions, and hypotheses; they are presented as the Truth.

In the classroom, what is the alternative to the Truth of the facts of arithmetic, the names and dates of history, and the rules of language? The alternative is opinion. As the problem of truth has filtered down into school life, it has been transformed into the familiar distinction between fact and opinion. All assertions, students learn (beginning in elementary school), can be classified either as fact or opinion. Fact statements possess truth-value: They refer to what might be called primary characteristics—to the nature of physical matter—and their truth-value can be determined by such means as weighing, measuring, counting, observing, and computing. Examples of fact statements (according to this school perspective) are "There are 12 people in this room"; "There is one gallon of chocolate ice cream in the container"; and "There are people called creationists or creation scientists who do not believe that the universe is billions of years old or that humankind evolved from other life forms."

Opinion statements do not possess truth-value: They refer to what might be called secondary characteristics—the realm of feeling and subjectivity—and they stand outside any system of verification. Even if someone offers justification, argument, or evidence in support of an opinion, the attempt can only be seen as persuasion, not proof. Examples of opinion statements are "The people in this room are kind"; "The chocolate ice cream in this container is delicious"; and "Creation science is a worthy belief."

Now, as I discussed earlier in this chapter, numerous difficulties result from this watered-down and flawed version of the problem of truth. Let me expand on these problems with an example of a supposedly "factual" statement (one that appeared on the quiz I discussed earlier): "George Washington was born on February 11, 1731." This is a fact statement because (in the language in which schoolchildren are instructed) it can be proved to be true or false. If someone wishes to object, saying that Washington was actually born on February 22, 1732, the objection does not change the nature of the assertion. The objector is merely observing that the original fact statement happens to be false. A third speaker might then note that both assertions about Washington's birth date are true, as the first states his birth date according to the calendar then in use, while the second states it according to our current calendar. Or it might be said that both statements are false, as neither provides enough information to explain what the stated date refers to.

This confusion about an apparently simple matter only begins to suggest the difficulties connected with the fact/opinion dichotomy. A much more serious difficulty is this: The assertions about Washington's birth date are said to be fact statements because they can be proved to be true or false. But how exactly would one prove the truth of either assertion? The issue here is not how we choose to designate or name the date in question, but rather how we know the temporal position of the event in question in sequence with other events. How can we be sure that we have fixed the correct point in the stream of time, regardless of the system we use to measure time? How can we know when George Washington was born?

Measuring, weighing, and observing are obviously irrelevant. Computing is useful only if we already know the point in time that we are trying to locate. The only proofs that can be offered for Washington's birth date are documents, in which case judgments must be made about the authenticity of the documents and about the reliability of those who produced them.

And this situation parallels that of creation science. The assertions of creation science—the fact statements—find their authority in documents. The constituent facts of creation science are offered with the same kind of proof one would offer to prove Washington's birth date. Within the scheme of the fact/opinion dichotomy, the assertions of creation science can only be disputed by challenging the interpretation of the documentary evidence. And the interpretation is an opinion, not a fact, which means that it lies outside any system of verification.

Some would like to argue that an irrefutable case has been made against "creation science." Judgments on this matter (and others like it) will pick out "intellectual rubbish," say Schick and Vaugn, if people follow "three simple rules" proposed by Bertrand Russell:

> (1) that when the experts are agreed, the opposite opinion cannot be held to be certain; (2) that when they are not agreed, no opinion can be regarded as certain by a nonexpert, and (3) that when they all hold that no sufficient grounds for a positive opinion exist, the ordinary man would do well to suspend his judgment. (Bertrand Russell, quoted in Schick & Vaughn, 2002, p. 104)

From this beginning, they tackle a number of different creationist assertions, countering (for example) "that no geological or anthropological evidence indicates that a worldwide flood occurred during the past ten thousand years," that "many of the rocks in the Earth's crust have been found to be billions of years old," that "present estimates put the age of the universe at something like 15 to 20 billion years," that "creatures all along the [evolutionary] continuum are alive today," that it is possible "for irreducibly complex systems to arise through natural selection," and that "biological evolution . . . has been observed many times over" (pp. 185–186, 189, 191–192). But these conclusions from the evidence, however compelling for many of us, can simply be dismissed by others as sloppy thinking and unpersuasive opinions.

Lesslie Newbigin also draws on Russell's notion of truth:

> In arriving at a scientific law there are three main stages: the first consists of observing the significant facts; the second in arriving at a hypothesis which, if it is true, would account for the facts; the third in deducing from this hypothesis consequences which can be tested by observation. (Bertrand Russell, quoted in Newbigin, 1989, p. 30)

Newbigin, taking what would seem to be the same stance on truth that Schick and Vaugn take, and drawing on the same evidence, comes to a conclusion precisely opposite to that of Schick and Vaugn: Evolutionary theory is untenable.

> A succession of scientists have pointed out enormous inconsistencies and impossibilities in the Darwinian theory of evolution by natural selection among random mutations. Cosmologists have affirmed that the known time-span of the universe is insufficient even for the earliest steps of this process. There is an almost total blank in many places where the intermediate stages between species should be represented in the fossil record. These and many other facts which seem to make the theory untenable are widely recognized. (Newbigin, 1989, p. 32)

Newbigin rejects, almost point by point, the conclusions that Schick and Vaugn find irrefutable—even though both sides claim to be working from the same evidence and to be applying to that evidence Russell's notion of truth as a correspondence between a mental occurrence and outside things (things that are understood by experts). Each side challenges the opinions of the other side and claims that the other side misunderstands the facts. They argue as if their truths were Truth that must be accepted by any sentient being, even though the unresolved dispute demonstrates that they possess no such Truth.

The school version of the problem of truth—some assertions are facts, the rest are opinions—makes it impossible to move from inquiry to Dewey's "warranted assertibility" or to satisfy Russell's search for the Truth. Creation science is one opinion; natural selection and the "Big Bang" are other opinions. Students are free to choose, but their choosing can only be a form of non-thinking because the terms of the distinction between fact and opinion make irrelevant any basis for the choice.

Some readers may wonder at this point if the problem of truth is like, say, the problem of traveling at the speed of light—that is, a genuine problem, perhaps, but one that doesn't come up much in the course of everyday activities. To consider that question, I want to look at how the problem of truth affects mathematics instruction in an elementary-school classroom.

THE PROBLEM OF TRUTH IN A MATHEMATICS CLASS

In *Teaching Problems and the Problems of Teaching*, Magdalene Lampert (2001) writes about teaching mathematics in a fifth-grade classroom. The deep background of this teaching comes (in part) from her "senior thesis in the philosophy of mathematics," which dealt with the "centuries-long argument about what it means to know that a mathematical statement is true" (p. 4). Writing about this background, Lampert explicitly acknowledges the significance of the problem of truth for teaching mathematics:

> Perhaps the most significant thing I learned from this work is that there are several different ways of thinking about why a mathematical statement is true, all reasoned and warranted. I observed that what it means to know something is a question that twentieth-century scholars can and do argue about. (pp. 4–5)

Because of her sensitivity to various approaches to mathematical reasoning, Lampert designed her instruction around problems that provided her students with something to reason about. In her class, "Learning . . . was a matter of becoming convinced that your strategy and your answer are mathematically legitimate" (p. 6)

Obviously this approach requires attention to "facts." The problems that were posed call for answers, and while different students reasoned in different ways to arrive at their answers, the students were still responsible for showing that an answer was "mathematically legitimate." But Lampert was more concerned with mathematical thinking than she was with right answers. She wanted her students to see that "multiple ideas, not right answers, were the 'coin of the realm' for buying attention" (p. 62). When she spoke with them, she didn't necessarily expect them to have "the right answer," but she did expect them to have an idea.

Beginning with the first lesson of the year, Lampert tried to communicate these expectations. In this lesson Lampert talked with the children about "revision" and about why she wanted them to write down all their thinking rather than erasing anything. She called on seven children, "asking them all to speak about the meaning of 'revision'" (p. 62). She wanted everyone in the class to see that they could all make "a useful contribution," so she wove the discussion out of the students' comments. In this way, both the manner of the discussion and its topic would reinforce the value of "multiple ideas."

But this deliberate strategy to deemphasize "right answers" (and avoid categorizing all statements as fact or opinion) did not eliminate such concerns from the students' thinking. Four of the seven children referred explicitly to right answers as an essential element of "revision."

Charlotte said, "You decide that maybe that's not the right, you don't think that that's the right idea and that you want to change it."

Shahroukh said, "Revision is when you have an idea and it's not correct."

Varouna said, "If you have an answer, wrong answer and then somebody has the right answer and you just might try to, like, revision it and get the right answer."

And Karim said, "Like the first time you thought it was the answer then you thought of it again and it was right" (pp. 62–63).

The students' intuition that problems in math classes have right answers is, it seems, on target. Later in the year, in a lesson following a quiz, the students were given this problem to work on:

Some people conjectured on the quiz that
$\frac{1}{2} + \frac{1}{6} = \frac{2}{8}$
Do you agree or disagree?
Write your reasoning.
Try to convince your group of what you think. (p. 341)

The use of the word *conjectured* is significant. At the beginning of the school year, Lampert had introduced the word, explaining that "a conjecture was a statement that had reasons behind it, but could be revised once it was discussed" (p. 72). The need for the special terminology should be clear from what I've already said in this chapter about the terms *fact* and *opinion*. Lampert wanted her students to see that a mathematical statement is supported by reasons (it isn't an "opinion"), but that even with those reasons, the statement is still open to discussion and revision (it isn't a "fact" or a "right answer"). The new term *conjecture* is necessary for a class of statements that is neither fact nor opinion.

And yet why is Lampert setting this problem for her students to reason about? We readers (as well as her students) are likely to suppose that she selected this problem as a way of correcting the common fifth-grader's misperception that fractions can be added by simply summing the numerators and then summing the denominators. The "people" who came up with the conjecture were reasoning that if $1 + 1 = 2$ and $2 + 6 = 8$, then $\frac{1}{2} + \frac{1}{6}$ must equal $\frac{2}{8}$. The implication of assigning this problem to reason about is that the "people" who made that conjecture were wrong, and that saying that they were wrong is something more than a conjecture—it's a fact.

Lampert does not spell out these implications. She does not ask her readers (and certainly not her students) if reasoning about a conjecture ever arrives at anything more than another conjecture. But her description of the discussion of this problem suggests that reasoning has the power to take the reasoner beyond conjecture, all the way, perhaps, to truth.

Tyrone, Lampert writes, "explained to me (and wanted to tell the whole class) what he was now thinking about [the problem]" (p. 340). So Tyrone sets out to explain what's wrong with the conjecture. Because "it was close to the end of the period" and Tyrone was "talking fast," his first stab at an explanation is awkward and confused. Lampert steps in to quiet the class and encourage Tyrone, and he tries again. But this time he has a different difficulty.

> TYRONE: One-sixth is the same as. What is it? One-twelfth.
> LAMPERT: Is one-sixth the same as one-twelfth?
> TYRONE: No.
> LAMPERT: No. I didn't think so. (pp. 340–341)

When Tyrone and Lampert agree that $\frac{1}{6}$ is not the same as $\frac{1}{12}$, are they making a conjecture? It doesn't seem so. This matter is settled, the statement so clearly true that Tyrone slaps himself in the forehead, as if to say, "How could I make such a mistake?"

After this misstep, however, Tyrone proceeds to offer his proof for why the conjecture under discussion is wrong. He says that $\frac{2}{8}$ is equal to $\frac{1}{4}$, a statement that is offered without argument. He then says that $\frac{1}{4}$ is less than $\frac{1}{2}$, another statement that is accepted without argument. He completes the proof by saying, "So if you add one-sixth to one-half it couldn't be two-eighths because two-eighths is smaller than one-half" (p. 341). At this point Lampert says (four times!), "Excellent," and we are told, "Many students applaud" (p. 342).

Tyrone's proof is constructed of what seem to be facts—namely, that fractions can be reduced according to certain procedures ($\frac{2}{8} = \frac{1}{4}$) and that when two fractions have a numerator of 1, the fraction with the larger denominator is the smaller number (¼ is less than ½). These statements do not seem to function as conjectures in the classroom; they do not need to be discussed.

The conclusion of the proof also seems to be something more than conjecture. Tyrone's reasoning has demonstrated and proved something. As shown by the responses of the teacher and of the rest of the students, they acclaim his achievement. Admittedly, their responses may reflect pleasure at the success of a student who has had difficulty with mathematics (on the quiz he left blank the items related to the conjecture he was now refuting), but the teacher and students clearly approve his reasoning. He has made a convincing case, and what would be the point of reasoning about a conjecture if the reasoning did not lead us to something more than another conjecture, if the reasoning did not convince us that this is indeed how things are? But while we can see that Tyrone's case persuades Lampert, the other fifth graders, and (probably) us readers, it is not so easy to see precisely how reasoning changes a conjecture into a truth.

The conjunction of facts and conjectures in Lampert's fifth-grade mathematics class indicates that the problem of truth has not been resolved by Lampert's emphasis on reasoning about mathematical statements. She recognizes that trying to classify a statement as either "fact" or "opinion" won't work and that disputes exist about how to prove the truth of a mathematical statement. She teaches her students how to reason about "conjectures," and she has them produce work that is more a record of thinking than an answer. And yet we still don't know why the statement "$\frac{1}{2} + \frac{1}{6} = \frac{2}{8}$" is a conjecture while the statement "$\frac{2}{8} = \frac{1}{4}$" is a fact. We can recognize from the way that people act that we have crossed some sort of boundary from a supposition to a certainty, but we still cannot say of what that boundary consists.

It might be supposed that because the problem I am talking about is unlikely ever to be raised in these terms by Lampert's students (or probably any other elementary-school students for that matter), teachers can safely ignore it. But even unspoken and ignored, the problem of truth affects the work that students do, shapes their notions of thinking, and can encourage non-thinking. Lampert herself provides an explicit example. In a chapter of her book in which she examines students' notebooks, she "zooms in" on Donna Ruth and Richard, and this is what she finds:

> In both Donna Ruth's and Richard's notebooks, the empty boxes are filled in with numbers that bear no relation to the mathematical task as set by the teacher. Perhaps one of them has "taught" the other that it is better to have the boxes filled in with *something* than to leave them empty, even if there is no clear reason for the numbers chosen, or perhaps they did not interpret the task

as having to do with multiplication. Can we say that these students were studying any mathematics? There is little evidence that the design of the problem
was productive of the kinds of constraints that would get them into worthwhile territory. (p. 130)

When Lampert asks if these students are "studying any mathematics,"
she poses a question that lies at the heart of my inquiry into the pursuit of
thinking in classrooms. She fears that what the students are doing is non-
thinking. How has this non-thinking happened? Opening up the process
of thinking (through the record in the notebooks) and providing objects of
thought (conjectures) were approaches that were supposed to ensure that
students would be reasoning about mathematics—that they would be thinking. Why didn't these approaches work?

One possible reason they didn't work is revealed when we look at the
situation from the point of view of Donna Ruth and Richard instead of that
of Lampert. I suspect that Donna Ruth and Richard would disagree with
Lampert when she says that "no clear reason" exists for them to write the
numbers they wrote in those boxes. I suspect that they feel that their reason
for completing this assignment in this way is as compelling as the reasoning
involved in many other assignments.

Their situation reminds me of another student observed in another classroom. Third graders at Benjamin Banniker Elementary School were presented
with the following problem: "Amber, Mario, Denise, and Jake have a pizza
they want to share fairly. How much pizza will each one get?" Tina counts
the names in the problem and announces her answer, "1, 2, 3, 4, so each
person would get two pieces of pizza" (Fleener, Carter, & Reeder, 2004,
p. 455). As teachers, we might be hesitant to accept Tina's assumption that
the pizza will necessarily be cut into eight pieces, but at least her reasoning
is clear and makes sense. The same cannot be said for Mary's reasoning,
however. After the teacher enters the discussion to move the children away
from thinking about numbers of pieces of pizza (as Tina did) and toward
thinking about fractions of a pizza, Mary announces her answer, "One and
a half; they're getting one and a half."

> TEACHER: [directed to Mary who has caught the teacher by surprise with
>   her unexpected answer] So if you have one pizza and each gets a fair
>   share . . .
> MARY: [Mary interrupts] One and a half.
> TEACHER: Baby, it's one pizza, not four. (pp. 455–456)

During the following 10 minutes (we are told by the observers of this
scene) Mary repeats her answer "One and a half," at least five times. Even
though from our point of view (that is, from the point of view of her teacher,

126   The Paradox of Believing

Fleener et al., and us readers) Mary's reasoning makes no sense, Mary seems to find it entirely sensible. Like Donna Ruth and Richard, she falls short of the teacher's expectation of thoughtfulness because she too fails to find in the problem "the kind of constraints" that would get her "into worthwhile territory."

Lampert's language seems to me to be deeply expressive of how the problem of truth undercuts thinking, and that word *constraints* invites further reflection. What it brings to my mind, when used in conjunction with the idea of getting "into worthwhile territory," is the activity of a collie herding sheep. Like the sudden dash and the bark of a herding dog, Lampert's "constraints" urge along her students' thoughts, preventing those thoughts (Lampert hopes) from getting caught in brambles or straying too far from water. The constraints hold the thoughts together and point them toward the territory where the grazing will be rewarding.

But of what, exactly, do these constraints consist?

The superficial answer is that Lampert hopes her students will be guided by facts; it is facts that constrain our thinking. If we know, for example, that $2/8 = \frac{1}{4}$ or that when two fractions have a numerator of 1, the fraction with the larger denominator is the smaller number, we are constrained when we go about creating mathematical conjectures. Knowing these kinds of things makes it impossible to insist (as Mary does) that when four children divide a pizza fairly, they will each get $1\frac{1}{2}$.

But unfortunately for Mary, Donna Ruth, Richard, and the rest of us as well, facts do not appear in the world with a suitable label attached. "No genuinely intellectual proposition," Dewey told us, "implies an assertion of its own truth" (Dewey, 1911/1998d, p. 117). Whatever assertion a statement makes is separate from the assertion that the statement is true. To say "four people dividing a pizza evenly each get $\frac{1}{4}$ of a pizza" is a different matter from saying "that statement about dividing the pizza is true," though in practice (and in math class) we tend to ignore the distinction. We know (or at least we think we do) what counts as "worthwhile territory" when one is doing mathematics, so we treat as fact in our teacherly reasoning what often seems to students to be merely conjecture (even if they have not been introduced to that term and the distinction it makes).

The problem is more blatant for Donna Ruth, Richard, and Mary, but it holds for other students as well. They cannot tell with certainty which elements of their thinking are facts and which are conjectures. They cannot tell when reasoning has produced an outcome that their teacher believes calls for further investigation and when it has produced an outcome that their teacher believes is final and persuasive.

The trouble, however, does not lie with the students. As the disputes between John Dewey and Bertrand Russell demonstrated, it lies in philosophy's inability to explain how anyone can arrive at the Truth. Logical systems can be devised to structure and guide reasoning, but they cannot prove (and are not intended to) that they produce the Truth. The acceptance of a line of reasoning as a certain pathway to the deep Truth of how things are is a separate matter from a judgment of its adequacy for the matter at hand.

THE PROBLEM OF TRUTH IN A FOUNDATIONS CLASS

Instances in which the problem of truth undermines classroom thinking are not limited to elementary school or to the study of mathematics. In some ways the problem of truth is even more corrosive when the subject matter is perceived as more a matter of opinion than of facts.

In an undergraduate foundations of education class I've taught for many years, one of our activities has sometimes been to read selections from Pamela Joseph and Gail Burnaford's book *Images of Schoolteachers in 20th-Century America*. We've focused especially on the ways in which popular-culture portrays teaching and teachers. We discuss the analyses of movies, television, and music that appear in the book and talk about whether these popular-culture portrayals enhance or hinder the education of those who are working to become teachers. Then I ask my students (preservice teachers) to think about a specific movie, piece of music, television program, or other work of culture and to write about what the portrayal of teaching in this work says about what it means to be a teacher in today's society. I also ask them to consider how this portrayal of teaching helps or hinders people who want to become teachers.

Mostly my students have written about movies. Their favorites (in the 1990s) were *Mr. Holland's Opus*, *Dangerous Minds*, *Dead Poets Society*, *Stand and Deliver*, and *Lean on Me*.

What happens next, after I critique the papers my students write, has been the most intriguing aspect of the assignment. When I critique their work, my students respond with uncharacteristic feeling. When I ask them if they intend to have their students stand on the desks and rip out pages from the front matter of textbooks (as they see and extol in *Dead Poet's Society*), they become uneasy with my insensitivity. When I ask them if force-feeding calculus (as they see and extol in *Stand and Deliver*) is truly an example of student-centered teaching, they find me querulous. When I ask if it is reasonable to expect teachers to sacrifice family and salary for the good of their students (as they see and extol in almost all of the movies), my students become indignant. For me even to ask such questions is an affront.

One student, discussing a revision of her paper, said to me, "I know you don't think that I should like this movie, but. . . ." In saying this, she put into words what I suspect was a common feeling among my students. She had watched a movie about her chosen profession—teaching. She had enjoyed the movie, admiring, and probably even being inspired by, the main character, and now she felt she was being told that her responses were somehow wrong. The professor doesn't think this is a good movie (she seemed to be saying), so she wasn't supposed to think so either. The irony of this is that I never told any of the students anything about the movies. I only asked questions. "Would you want to let a student stay in your home?" "Do you plan to reward students with trips to expensive restaurants?" "Do you think all teachers should ignore a doctor's advice to take it easy?"

Why were these inquiries perceived to be so threatening?

To think about this question, it may help to look at a few brief excerpts from the papers. These aren't from the best papers that I received, but they capture elements common to most of the papers.

> This movie clearly displays what it means to be a teacher. The teacher had such a wonderful experience with his class.

> The teacher demonstrates a great deal of patience by dealing with both his problems as well as his students' problems.

> The teacher shows a great deal of knowledge of the curriculum.

> It seemed as if the students gained confidence from the teacher, because he made his instruction clear and easy for them to understand.

> The teacher showed a great deal of compassion for his students.

> By supporting the students, the teacher shows that the students are able to think for themselves.

Of all of the qualities that these excerpted student comments reveal about the papers, there is one in particular about which I want to comment—the faceless generality of the portraits. Here are the movies discussed in these comments—*Mr.Holland's Opus, Dangerous Minds, Dead Poets Society, Stand and Deliver*, and *Lean on Me*. Which movie was the student talking about in the following excerpt? "By supporting the students, the teacher shows that the students are able to think for themselves." Or in this one? "The teacher demonstrates a great deal of patience by dealing with both his problems as well as his students' problems." I admit that I have increased the facelessness of these comments by plucking them from their context and by removing the names and inserting instead the words "the teacher." Changing the words may not be playing fair, but my point is that when the names are removed, readers cannot tell which movie is being discussed, not even if the readers are thoroughly familiar with the movies.

This inability to identify which movie the writers are commenting on is especially surprising when the nature of the comments is considered. These students are enunciating their big ideas about what the movies say about teaching. The topics are not trivial. A teacher who helps students think for themselves deserves admiration. Such an outcome is one of the highest aims of teaching and worthy of dramatic treatment. But saying that a teacher in a movie achieves this doesn't help pick out one movie from a group because in the movies every good teacher (according to my students) helps students think for themselves. It doesn't matter whether the movie is about John Keating teaching his private-academy students to "seize the day" by ripping the introduction out of their literature books, or about LouAnne Johnson teaching her inner-city students to take English class seriously by showing them some karate moves, or about principal Joe Clark instituting a new school regime by throwing out the troublemakers. Regardless of what they teach or how they teach it, all the good teachers in the movies come out looking the same—or at least they look enough alike to my students that characterizations of the teachers are indistinguishable.

The reason for the faceless generality of these portrayals of teachers in the movies is that, from my students' point of view, all that really matters is that these are "good teachers." Why my students believe them to be "good teachers" is irrelevant (and may not be expressible) because the judgment (they would say) is an opinion.

There are no "facts" to be weighed in the recognition of a "good teacher." The specifics of the teaching are irrelevant, and this is why my students react so indignantly to my questions about the assertions they make in their papers. I am asking questions about the facts of the movies, and the facts don't matter. From my students' point of view, the assignment is a matter of opinion, and for me to question their opinion is not playing by the rules. They are (they would probably like to say) entitled to their opinion. Aeon J. Skoble has argued that a vaguely stated but deeply rooted belief in the sanctity of opinions permeates our society. Television talk shows and newspapers promote the opinions of experts, but viewers and readers tend to believe that "their opinions, their perspectives, are just as worthwhile," an attitude that is "based on the underlying (if unstated) premise that 'No one really knows anything' or 'It's all a matter of opinion and mine counts too.'" Skoble worries especially about this rationale. "If it were true that everything were merely a matter of opinion, then it actually would follow that mine is as relevant as the expert's; indeed there would be no such thing as expertise" (Skoble, in Irwin, Conrad, & Skoble, 2001, p. 25).

The devastating effects on thinking of the denial of expertise are explored in Schick and Vaughn's (2002) book *How to Think About Weird Things: Critical Thinking for a New Age*. Schick and Vaughn set out to debunk a variety of "weird" beliefs, from ESP to UFOs to the topic I discussed earlier in this chapter—"creation science." At the heart of their critique are the "three simple rules" proposed by Bertrand Russell. Each rule depends upon the concept of expertise and upon agreement about who the experts are. Without acceptance of both the existence of experts and a general agreement about who the experts are, no opinion can have precedence over another. But the possibility of expert opinion is undercut by a strict division between fact and opinion, which implies that expertise can be related only to facts. Questions of which facts to attend to, which facts to believe, what to do about or with the facts, as well as who counts as an expert, are all matters of opinion—a realm necessarily outside expertise.

With an issue as obviously based on opinion as the question of how one responds to a movie, my students understandably feel that the rules have changed when I try to pin down their assertions in ways that seem to rely on facts. How can there be truth and expertise in an endeavor such as movie watching that is so clearly a matter of opinion? More than one student complained to me that she didn't see how I could grade the assigned paper, because I would have to grade her opinion, and I couldn't do that; it wouldn't be right.

I have tried to rebut such challenges to the assignment and to establish the possibility of categories of thought that transcend the simplistic differentiation of fact and opinion. I have argued, for example, that sometimes an opinion doesn't bear scrutiny. Take, for example, the student who wrote, "This movie clearly displays what it means to be a teacher. The teacher had such a wonderful experience with his class." The student was writing about John Keating in *Dead Poets Society*. In other words, the suicide of one of Keating's students and Keating's subsequent firing were being characterized as "a wonderful experience." Surely (I argue) this opinion is a silly trivializing of what the movie is about. This cannot be (I want to say) what the movie means. And yet I know that that may be precisely what it means to at least one viewer. Caught in the toil of the problem of truth, my students and I find it almost impossible to talk about the ways in which our world tells us what it means to be a teacher. All we can do is present our opinions and then fall silent.

MEANING AND TRUTH

I would like at this point to be able to say, "Here is what teachers should do to make sure that thinking in classrooms is not thwarted by a dichotomy of fact and opinion." Unfortunately, the problem of truth is not a question to be answered, and it has no solution. It is instead a way of saying that we are beings trapped within a perpetual struggle between embedded habits of mind and an insatiable appetite for questions. From the moment of birth, we test the world, finding out what will happen if we drop this spoon, mix these colors, drink this liquid, turn this corner, read this book, marry this person. But the questions themselves point toward the sense that there is something that is not questions, something that holds these questions together. Victor Kestenbaum asks, "[W]hat ideals will motivate the struggle, give it—and the agent—potency, elevation, depth? In other words, 'in the midst of effort,' in the midst of the perturbation and conflict, what is there?" For an answer, Kestenbauum turns to Dewey:

> In *Human Nature and Conduct*, Dewey calls it "the sense of an enveloping whole." And it is in *Art as Experience* that he calls it "the deep-seated memory of an underlying harmony, the sense of which haunts life like the sense of being founded on a rock." (Kestenbaum, 2002, p. 57)

We yearn for meaning to bring harmony to our scattered lives, meaning that transcends shifting truths and finds the rock of Truth. This ancient yearning has been attributed to Socrates as a desire to think "whole thoughts," to find that which is "absolutely true, being the very principles according to which God governs the world" (Davidson, 1892/1969, p. 134). Like Socrates, we yearn for "whole thoughts," but thinking leads (for us, as it did for Socrates) always to questions and conjectures.

Observing the vacuity of classroom discussions when "moral and existential questions" are banished, Katherine Simon treats the problem of engaging students in meaningful questions as a curriculum problem. She offers "strategies and tools for incorporating moral and existential questions into the classroom," discussing units, lessons, assessment, and teacher collaboration (2001, pp. 232–248). Among the strategies is the injunction to "*Support students in developing an informed opinion*" (p. 237). This, it seems to me, would be excellent advice—provided we could first agree about what an "informed opinion" is. How much information is necessary to turn an ordinary opinion into one that is informed? What kind of information is necessary? How much and what kind of information would a viewer of a movie about teaching need to possess in order to generate an informed opinion? And when informed opinions clash, is it because one is more informed than another? How can Magdalene Lampert's mathematics students know when their conjectures (their opinions) are sufficiently informed?

The problem at the heart of these questions is that the words *informed* and *opinion* cannot be combined into an intelligible phrase as long as the problem of truth is reduced to a dichotomization of fact and opinion. The words *fact* and *opinion* attach more clearly to different kinds of purposes than to different kinds of statements. We use *fact* when we are interested in verification, validity, legitimation of belief. We use *opinion* when we are interested in connection, significance, continuity, meaning. Most of what we say involves both interests simultaneously.

The shift in our understanding of *fact* and *opinion* from statements to purposes turns our attention from truth to meaning. The price of this shift is that we must relinquish our claim to the capital-*T* Truths that provide Russell's "rest and peace."

We can (and I believe we should) try to create classrooms where we value meaning at least as much as we value truth, where children spend more time talking about their reasoning about math problems than they do talking about the answers. Otherwise, we force our students to live in a world where all language boils down to one category called "facts" and another called "opinions," and we create an environment of non-thinking. Facts do not need to be thought about, only recalled. Opinions do not need to be thought about, only embraced. Thinking becomes inconceivable.

Can we avoid this end? I believe we can, and to support my belief I want to take up the notion of "thinking for one's self," the topic of Chapter 6.

Thinking for Oneself

The phrase "think for one's self" is a pleonasm. Unless one does it for one's self, it isn't thinking.

—John Dewey, *Democracy and Education*

For more than a decade now I have been asking graduate students in my course on the history and philosophy of education to read Dewey's *Democracy and Education*. They have stumbled over, wrestled with, ignored, and outright rejected many passages in that book, but I have never known a student to be puzzled by or question the sentences quoted above. Obviously, thinking is something each of us does on our own for ourselves. We cannot think someone else's thoughts.

The redundancy of the phrase is so obvious, in fact, that it makes me wonder not only why people talk about "thinking for one's self" but also why Dewey feels obliged to point out the redundancy of the phrase. How can the matter ever have been in doubt?

In this chapter I want to explore the notion of thinking for one's self and to argue that it is not as obvious or as easy as it seems. Although the phrase sounds unambiguously self-evident, it harbors a puzzle: Thinking (which is private and personal) somehow leads to thoughts (which are public and sharable). If the products of our thinking belonged to us individually (affecting neither other beings nor the world in which we live) they would be useless. When we think for our selves, we are also thinking for others. But how does this work? I'm going to begin to explore this puzzle by looking more closely at what Dewey said about "thinking for one's self" and thinking (myself) about why he said it.

THE INDIVIDUALITY OF THINKING

Dewey's comment on "thinking for one's self" appears in chapter 22 of *Democracy and Education*, "The Individual and the World." There is, Dewey says, an "assumed antithesis between purely individualistic methods of learning and social action, and between freedom and social control" (p. 301). We assume (wrongly, according to Dewey) that the child's impulses are necessarily at odds with the purposes of the school. In fact, Dewey says, the school is the place where the effects of assuming this antithesis are most clearly reflected, being revealed "in the absence of a social atmosphere and motive for learning" and then in the separation that arises "between method of instruction and methods of government" (p. 301).

It is within this discussion of how an "assumed antithesis" between "freedom and social control" warps school life that Dewey touches upon thinking.

> Individuality as a factor to be respected in education has a double meaning. In the first place, one is mentally an individual only as he has his own purpose and problem, and does his own thinking. The phrase "think for one's self" is a pleonasm. Unless one does it for one's self, it isn't thinking. Only by a pupil's own observations, reflections, framing and testing of suggestions can what he already knows be amplified and rectified. Thinking is as much an individual matter as is the digestion of food. (1916/1966 pp. 302–303)

The case here is that individuality is an important factor in education and that one of the reasons for this is that thinking is (in some ways, at least) an individual matter. Now, what is it that makes thinking "an individual matter"?

In just these few sentences, Dewey offers three takes on the individuality of thinking. First, thinking is individual because it has to do with "purpose and problem"; second, it is individual because it consists of "observations, reflections, framing and testing of suggestions" in order to amplify and rectify what is already known; and third, the individuality of thinking is exemplified by an analogy between thinking and digesting. None of these characterizations is quite as straightforward as it seems, and I want to look more closely at each.

MAKING A PROBLEM ONE'S OWN

When does a problem or purpose become my own? Does the second grader (from Chapter 4), trying to figure out how many houses Godzilla smashed, have a problem of her own? How about Mary (from Chapter 5), who is trying to convince her classmates that if four children share a pizza, each one will get "1½"? Cases like these, in which the problem is initially set by a teacher and then presented to a student, do not seem to fit the criterion of having one's own purpose, and yet these children do seem to be taking up the problem as if it were their own. I recall one of my graduate students saying that left on her own, she would never have read *Democracy and Education*, but that having been obliged because of the course requirements to read and discuss the book, she was glad she had done it: It changed how she thought about her teaching. I suspect that this is not an unusual occurrence in classrooms. After all, education is often thought of in terms of expanding a student's horizon. Many students probably find that the teacher's problem becomes their problem.

However, there are instances when a student originates a problem, but it is still doubtful that we would say the student has her own problem and purpose. Consider the undergraduate student (from Chapter 5) who argues in an essay that John Keating (in *Dead Poets Society*) has a "wonderful experience" with his students. Although the essay assignment is not the student's invention, the claim that the essay makes does originate with the student. But in this student's mind, the claim presents nothing problematic. There is no thinking necessary to make the claim; it is simply an opinion that exists, requiring (so the student supposes) neither evidence nor interpretation nor analysis. The claim is an ersatz problem.

The question of when a problem is the student's own cannot be answered by reporting on who originates the problem. But how, then, can a teacher tell when a problem or purpose becomes a student's own?

An answer to this question is dramatically sketched in the W. E. B. Du Bois story "Of the Coming of John," from the book *The Souls of Black Folk*. Du Bois tells the post–Civil War story of John Jones, a "long, straggling fellow . . . brown and hard-haired" known both for his awkwardness and his "bubbling good nature and genuine satisfaction with the world." John goes off to school, to the Wells Institute, and his family looks forward to the day when he will return. That day, they are sure, will be filled with parties and "speakings in the churches." There will be "new furniture in the front room" and a "new schoolhouse, with John as teacher." But the White folk shake their heads and say of his schooling, "It'll spoil him,—ruin him" (Du Bois, 1903/1990, p. 166).

In his first term at the institute, John is "loud and boisterous, always laughing and singing" (p. 167), and he is suspended before the first term is up. The suspension shocks him, and he determines to make a success of himself. Allowed to return at the beginning of the following term, he comes back "with sober eyes and a set and serious face" (p. 168).

Learning comes hard for him, "but all the world toward which he strove was of his own building." He pushes himself to see

> beyond the world of men into a world of thought. And the thoughts at times puzzled him sorely; he could not see just why the circle was not square, and carried it out fifty-six decimal places one midnight,—and would have gone further, indeed, had not the matron rapped for lights out. He caught terrible colds lying on his back in the meadows of nights, trying to think out the solar system; he had grave doubts as to the ethics of the Fall of Rome, and strongly suspected the Germans of being thieves and rascals, despite his text-books; he pondered long over every new Greek word, and wondered why this meant that and why it couldn't mean something else, and how it must have felt to think all things in Greek. (p. 168).

In this passage Du Bois paints a portrait of a student who has his own problems and purposes. John's professors pose questions about mathematics and astronomy and history and Greek; they teach John that if a fraction can be written to represent the area of a circle, the same fraction cannot equal the area of a square; that the planets move across the night sky in predictable rhythms; that the corruption of Rome led to its collapse; that ἐγκύκλιοι is the Greek word for the "liberal" arts. And to every teaching John responds, "Why?" and asks himself if these matters really must be understood as the professors have portrayed them. He agonizes at every step.

The John Jones who graduates from the institute and eventually returns to the muddy little town in the South is a different man from the one who left. When he tries to speak to family and friends, he finds himself unable to communicate. At the "meeting of welcome at the Baptist church," he talks about "new ideas," about the "rise of charity and popular education." He asks "what part the Negroes of this land would take in the striving of the new century," sketches a plan for a "new Industrial School," and urges people to set aside "religious and denominational bickering" (p. 173). But none of this talk means anything to the people he is speaking to. "Little had they understood of what he said, for he spoke an unknown tongue" (p. 174). He had become educated, and he was no longer one of them.

After the meeting, John talks to his sister in a passage that speaks with profound insight into teaching and learning.

> "John," she said, "does it make every one unhappy when they study and learn lots of things?"
>> He paused and smiled. "I am afraid it does," he said.
>> "And, John, are you glad you studied?"
>> "Yes," came the answer, slowly but positively. (p. 174)

There is more to the tale Du Bois tells of John Jones, but the portion I have related illustrates the answer I have in mind to that question of what it is that signifies that a school problem has become the student's own problem. Thinking does not settle anything; it unsettles. To take on a problem as our own is to embrace uncertainty. To take on a problem as our own is to become changed in unpredictable ways. So great is the change in John that at the end of the story he momentarily forgets who he himself had been: "[H]e thought of the boys at Johnstown. He wondered how Brown had turned out, and Carey? And Jones,—Jones? Why, *he* was Jones" (p. 179). That long, straggling, good-natured fellow belongs in someone else's life because the problems that the man John has struggled with and grown through have annihilated and almost erased from memory the boy who was Jones.

Becoming unsettled (or numbed, as Meno said of the effect of Socrates) and the change that accompanies this disorder are signs of our taking on a problem as our own. They also point toward some of the reasons for non-thinking to be so attractive. "[N]on-thinking," says Hannah Arendt, "seems so recommendable a state for political and moral affairs"—precisely the sorts of affairs that make up much of classroom life (1978, p. 177). It shields "people from the dangers of examination," the primary danger being of course the perplexity that results from thinking. The unsettling nature of thinking leads always to the temptation to call an end to thinking. This temptation, described by Arendt as the "ever-present danger of thinking," arises "out of the desire to find results that would make further thinking unnecessary" (1978, pp. 176–177). When we have taken on a problem as our own, the power of thinking to unsettle and unnerve us makes us eager to solve the problem, and so bring an end to thinking.

OBSERVATIONS, REFLECTIONS, FRAMING, AND TESTING

The second way in which Dewey described thinking as an individual matter is that a "pupil's own observations, reflections, framing and testing of suggestions" are required if the pupil is to "amplify" and "rectify" what is already known. What Dewey has in mind seems to be what he calls (in *School and Society*) "realizing" an interest "through its direction" (1902/1990, p. 40). He describes the drawing of a 7-year-old at the University School:

> They had been talking [in class] about the primitive conditions of social life when people lived in caves. The child's idea of that found expression in this way: the cave is neatly set up on the hillside in an impossible way. You see the conventional tree of childhood—a vertical line with horizontal branches on

each side. If the child had been allowed to go on repeating this sort of thing day by day, he would be indulging his instinct rather than exercising it. But the child was now asked to look closely at trees, to compare those seen with the one drawn, to examine more closely and consciously into the conditions of his work. Then he drew trees from observation.

Finally he drew again from combined observation, memory, and imagination. He made again a free illustration, expressing his own imaginative thought, but controlled by detailed study of actual trees. (pp. 40, 43)

The picture that results from the comparisons and observations, Dewey writes, is a scene with "as much poetic feeling as the work of an adult" (p. 43). This achievement is possible because the criticism of the boy's first attempt arises from his own comparisons, observations, and reflections. Instead of working from instructions about how to sketch a tree or standards for the artistic development of 7-year-olds, the boy weighs his drawing (and his idea of what the drawing is to accomplish) against the trees he sees, seeing them now as reflections upon his artwork.

The boy's observation and response call to mind the "two-in-one" that Hannah Arendt says "Socrates discovered as the essence of thought" (1978, p. 185). When we are thinking, argues Arendt, we are engaged in an internal dialogue. "It is this *duality* of myself with myself," she says, "that makes thinking a true activity, in which I am both the one who asks and the one who answers" (p. 185). When the boy asks what his picture is supposed to be, what it is supposed to do, how he would know if it was a good picture, it is himself who answers. He questions himself.

When he then turns from this internal dialogue and attends to and acts upon his picture, Arendt would say that his thinking has ended. "The faculty of judging particulars (as brought to light by Kant)," she writes, "the ability to say, 'this is wrong,' 'this is beautiful,' and so on, is not the same as the faculty of thinking" (p. 193). Arendt's use of the terms *thinking* and *judging* is at odds with usage that makes evaluating (or judging) a dimension of thinking (as in Bloom's *Taxonomy*, for example), but the distinction she makes is a more important matter than how words are defined. There is an activity (she calls it "thinking") that involves a moving away from action and away from (echoing Plato's myth of the cave) the world of appearances. When the fruits of that activity are turned to account in the world of appearances (when the boy concludes, say, that his picture needs to be more realistic), there is a return.

The theme of "withdrawal-and-return" is described by Arnold Toynbee as the "mystic path" taken by "creative personalities" as they move "first out of action into ecstasy and then out of ecstasy into action again" (1962, p. 248). Like Arendt, Toynbee sees the movement of withdrawal-and-return epitomized in Plato's myth of the cave, but he traces it as well in the stories of 27 individuals (from Confucius, Saint Paul, and Muhammad to Dante and Hamlet), in the cycle of seasons, and in puberty rites. The ubiquity of the theme suggests that experience of it is not limited to "creative personalities" and that it is in fact the pattern of creativity. It is, I believe, another version of the thinking that Arendt identifies as the two-in-one.

What does all this say about the individuality of thinking insofar as it arises from the "pupil's own observations, reflections, framing and testing of suggestions"? As a withdrawal from action (or from the world of appearances), Dewey's "observations, reflections, framing and testing" occur in that peculiar solitude where the self encounters itself. This sort of thinking "deals with invisibles, with representations of things that are absent" (Arendt, 1978, p. 193). When Dewey's 7-year-old examines "more closely and consciously into the conditions of his work," he is turning not toward the paper that lies on the table in front of him, but toward something that is absent—toward an idea of what the lines on that paper might become.

The conditions of teachers' work make it necessary, however, to focus on that which is present, on action and the world of appearances. "Thinking which is not connected with increase of efficiency in action," writes Dewey, "and with learning more about ourselves and the world in which we live, has something the matter with it just as thought" (1916/1966, p. 152). Teachers cannot be satisfied with having their students retreat into the solitude of thinking. Even if the withdrawal from action is valued, the return is the payoff. A "reflective experience" or a "complete act of thought" (as described by Dewey) begins with the "perplexity, confusion, doubt" associated with "an incomplete situation" and is only consummated with "doing something overtly to bring about the anticipated result" (p. 150).

The problem is that with an emphasis on results, the internal dialogue of thinking begins to be seen as unnecessary. The need to have students do something, to bring about a result—draw a picture, write an essay, produce an answer to a question—encourages teachers to bypass the withdrawal from action and to assume that the doing is all that really matters. If a student produces the right answers, if she turns in a mechanically correct and factually accurate essay, we conclude not only that we have done a good job of teaching but also that the student has done a good job of thinking. In fact, as long as the instructional aim of schooling is simply to turn out students who can pass the tests, the internal dialogue of "myself with myself" is irrelevant.

We may even begin to see "thinking" as something unreal. William C. Dement, a sleep researcher, tells several stories about individuals (one of them himself) whose lives changed because of a dream. One person dreams about getting lung cancer and quits smoking; another dreams about being unhappily married to Jim and marries Mike instead; a third dreams about an "awful time" as a student at the University of California at Berkeley and decides to enroll at Stanford. Dement comments, "To some it may seem amazing that people will take drastic action as a result of something that didn't even happen. But the emotional impact of dreams can be so powerful that they might as well really have occurred" (Dement & Vaughan, 1999, p. 293).

I want to argue that the dream *is* something that really occurred and that the experience of the dream is as real as the experience in a doctor's office or at a wedding or in a college class. Now, I am not saying that dreaming and thinking are identical, but thinking-as-internal-dialogue shares some of the qualities of dreaming. Both exhibit the pattern of withdrawal-and-return, and both illustrate "the duality of myself with myself." And there are those who will say of both thinking and dreaming that this is "something that didn't even happen."

By denying the reality of "the duality of myself with myself," thinking-as-internal-dialogue comes to be seen as a waste of time. The "pupil's own observations, reflections, framing and testing of suggestions" are valid and desirable only if they conform to curricular plans and teacher expectations. Otherwise, thinking is too individual a matter, and non-thinking is preferable.

AS INDIVIDUAL AS DIGESTION

The most provocative of Dewey's three characterizations of the individuality of thinking is the comparison with digestion. Admittedly, Dewey does not say that thinking works the way that digestion works, only that thinking is as individual as digestion. Nevertheless, it is a remarkable assertion.

Digestion is an individual matter, in part, because each of us performs the task with our own equipment. My teeth chew my food and no one else's. My stomach juices work only on what I eat. In the same way, presumably, each of us performs the tasks of thinking with our own equipment. The neuronal network of my brain connects to no one else's body. The thinking of a school student is done with her brain and not with her teacher's or some other student's.

All this is obvious, but digestion is an individual matter in another sense as well. What I eat cannot be eaten by someone else. Another person can eat a slice of lasagna cut from the same casserole dish that my slice came from, but no one else can eat the slice I ate. Is thinking individual in this sense too? If I think a thought and give it shape (in language, music, paint, film, or action), does it become impossible for someone else who has encountered my thought to think the same thought?

At first glance, it may seem that the answer to these questions has to be an unambiguous "Of course not!" If the most salient measure of school accountability is whether students can answer certain questions, it seems reasonable to suppose that the popular opinion is that all these students (who pass the test) are thinking the same thoughts.

But the popular opinion is not as unambiguous as that. In fact, strong support for the assertion that two people cannot think the same thought can be found in our school policies regarding plagiarism.

While plagiarism has long been a matter of concern in schools, the concern has grown substantially with the increasing availability of the Internet. The National Center for Education Statistics estimates (on their Web page!) that at the end of 2001, 99% of U.S. public schools were linked to the Internet (2004). Nearly all schoolchildren have at their fingertips access to an inexhaustible fund of information, ready to be cut and pasted into their latest assignment. It's not surprising that my Internet search of the phrase "plagiarism detection" in January 2004 produced more than 15,000 sites. They ranged from those of businesses selling software to detect plagiarism to university sites with advice on the subject of avoiding academic dishonesty to sites for "paper mills" offering students "assistance" with their writing assignments.

One of these sites, written by a university librarian, offers "strategies to deter academic misconduct." After discussing the ease with which students can retrieve "full text information ready to be copied" and the need for "university policy on plagiarism," Mary Hricko (2004) argues that "it is important that we teach [students] how to cite their references," that student assignments should allow students to use the Internet only "for reference materials," and that students should be helped to "develop their paraphrasing skills." These policies will help deter academic misconduct, Hricko believes, because "in most situations, plagiarism occurs as a result of ignorance."

Hricko's position is, in part, supported at a Web page sponsored by Turnitin, a company selling a plagiarism-detection service. Technology has muddied the concept of plagiarism, says Turnitin, and made the act of plagiarizing seem benign:

> The seemingly "public" nature of online content blurs the distinction between publicly and privately owned information. Electronic resources, by nature easily reproducible, are not perceived as "intellectual property" in the same way that their material counterparts are. Just as file transfer programs such as Napster make it easy to trade copyrighted music files most people would never think to steal in physical form, the Internet makes plagiarism easy for students who might have thought twice about copying from a book or published article. (Plagiarism.org, 2004.)

For Turnitin as for Hricko, plagiarism is (for the most part) an oversight, a forgetting, a misunderstanding. A student finds some text appearing on the screen of her own computer, and she comes to think of it as her own.

I have known students who defended borrowing from the Internet by saying that they didn't copy it from a book; it was on the Web. I grappled with this problem myself as I tried to figure out if I needed permission from a publisher to reprint the stanza from a poem of Robert Frost that appears in Chapter 3. When I did an online search using a line from the poem, "I have been one acquainted with the night," more than 1,500 Web sites were identified. That is, at each of those 1,500 sites at least one line of the poem was quoted, and, in fact, the entire poem was quoted at all the sites I visited. One site even claimed that the poem was believed to be in the public domain, which is not true. Only one site that I inspected indicated that permission to use the poem had been granted. Finding this poem freely circulating in the ether of the Internet, one might well wonder (as I did), whose poem it is. But this is a legal problem about the fair use of copyrighted material, not an issue of academic dishonesty.

So why is plagiarism counted as a form of academic dishonesty? What exactly is the educational crime of plagiarism? Surprisingly few Web sites that discuss plagiarism ask such questions. Hricko and Turnitin seem to be saying that the crime is the failure to give proper attribution and that students who plagiarize are stealing ideas and therefore injuring the owner, but this conclusion is not spelled out. Another Web site offers somewhat different reasons for thinking of plagiarism as a crime that educators need to discourage: "Apart from discrediting the use of assignments for assessment, the copying of assignments also vitiates the assignments' educational aims" ("Plagiarism Detection—YAP," 2004). Here two different kinds of wrong are named. When students plagiarize, they make it impossible for a teacher to assess their work, and the students themselves miss out on the learning they ought to have experienced.

What none of the sites I looked at said (perhaps because it is too obvious) is that copying a passage is not the same as thinking the ideas. This is why copying "vitiates . . . educational aims," why it discredits "the use of assignments for assessment," why it counts as a kind of stealing, why we put quotation marks around other people's words. If writing or saying words were the same as thinking the thoughts embodied by the words, plagiarism would not be a form of academic dishonesty (though it still might involve copyright infringement). But reciting Hamlet's most famous soliloquy does not require contemplating suicide; copying Lincoln's "Gettysburg Address" does not require agonizing over civil war. Using someone else's words is not an instance of the internal dialogue of thinking.

When we quote something (whether directly or indirectly, in writing or in speech), the quoted material has a different status from that of the words in which it is embedded. Conventions exist to indicate this status—commas; quotation marks; introductory words or phrases such as *that* or *so called*;

and (in speech) pausing or changing emphasis, tone, or dialect. But these conventions were created to mark a state that exists even when the conventions are not used. Quotation existed before quotation marks were invented. When quoted material is not conventionally set off from the words in which it is embedded, it is still quoted material, even though readers or listeners may not be aware of where the writer's or speaker's words leave off and the quoted material begins. That is, readers or listeners may not recognize when the text—which represents internal dialogue and manifests the two-in-one—is interrupted by the importation of external material.

Plagiarism is academic dishonesty because a student who says "to be or not to be" or "government of the people, by the people, and for the people" is not thinking those words, she is quoting them, and if she fails to acknowledge her borrowing, she is attempting to deceive. The sense of indignation that plagiarism arouses begins with the belief that once a thought has been expressed, it becomes impossible for someone else to think that thought in just those words. Thinking is as individual as digestion. Once Lincoln has pondered the essence of democratic government in his terms, the rest of us can try to digest a slice like the one he's chewed over, but we cannot digest that slice. When we say those words, "government of the people, by the people, and for the people," we bring to mind the whole of Lincoln's story, the turbulent years that led to civil war, the terrible battle at Gettysburg, and a long history since that battle that formed no part of Lincoln's internal dialogue. We can think about what Lincoln thought, but we cannot think what he thought, and to pretend otherwise is academic dishonesty—it is plagiarism.

Now, there is certainly some non-thinking involved in the act of plagiarism. A student who attempts to fulfill an essay assignment by copying a Web page and putting her name on it is not thinking the content of the paper that she presents as her own. But ironically, even more pervasive and debilitating forms of non-thinking arise from the efforts typically advocated to prevent plagiarism.

The advice given by Hricko (above) summarizes the usual approaches for deterring this form of academic dishonesty: Teach students the proper forms of citation, insist that research should provide only "reference materials," and help students become more skilled at paraphrasing. The advice sounds tried and true, but what do students learn from these lessons?

To begin with, they learn that quoted material is acceptable in their writing if it is surrounded by the appropriate markings. They discover that the use of a particular system of citation (APA or MLA or Chicago or a school's "house style") renders quoted material safe for inclusion in their work. I have not conducted a survey to find out how students explain the magical power of citation, but I suspect that the common explanation would be that citation shows where the information came from and (perhaps more important) that it shows that the information is to be trusted. If John Dewey says, "Unless one does it for one's self, it isn't thinking," the claim is presumed to have some merit because Dewey is an expert about such things. Proper citation (students may believe) makes the quoted matter more valuable and the paper more intellectually weighty and persuasive.

Hricko's second method of combating plagiarism—restrict quotations to "reference materials" (especially when students are quoting from the Internet)—is intended to remind students that facts do not speak for themselves. Information needs to be interpreted and shaped into an argument, and while online sources and books and journals can provide the information, the student must provide the interpretation and the shaping. But embedded in this perspective is the strict distinction between fact and opinion that I critiqued in Chapter 5. Because "reference materials" are seen as the facts of the matter, telling students that they can use Web sites to gather only "reference materials" reinforces the idea that quotation (when it is properly cited) provides writing with intellectual force. The message is further reinforced when teachers require students to use 5 or 10 or 20 sources of various designations—so many books, so many journals, so many online sites. The weight of the sources seems to be directly correlated to the worth of the paper, and the student's role in the preparation of the mélange is that of editor or anthologist. The thinking required of the student is limited to recognizing which sources to include, for the issues have already been defined by the "reference materials." Often, because of the nature of the assignment, students are incompetent to make any further contribution. A high-school student from the Midwest in the United States who has been asked to write about resolving civil strife in Liberia can do little more than trust the experts. An elementary-school student from Atlanta who is to write a report about tigers in India can undoubtedly come up with information, along with full-color pictures, but even so she is ill prepared to think about tigers in India.

The debilitating effects on thinking that result from dependence on "reference materials" to provide intellectual weight are especially evident in academia. At a university faculty-development program, I heard a professor offer several strategies for helping students become critical thinkers. Reading the list of instructional strategies from a PowerPoint slide, he added that these were not methods he had come up with on his own, that they were instead methods that had been written about "in the literature." This instinctive effort at citation served but one purpose—to lend weight to his presentation. The value of the methods, he was implying, lay in their citability.

And, he might well ask, why not? Isn't it true that intellectual weight in academic writing depends on references and sources? Why, he could demand, does this book have a bibliography? Are you, the professor might challenge me, any more competent to write about thinking and non-thinking than the high-school student was to write about civil strife in Liberia or the elementary-school student was to write about tigers in India? Or are you just as dependent as they are on references and sources?

One response to these questions is that if we value thinking, we evaluate writing or speaking by the cogency of its argument and the insight it provides, not by the number or sources of its citations. If we value thinking, we treat quotation (or "reference materials") not as the conclusion that resolves a problem, but as itself a problem that calls for reflection. When I began this chapter with a quotation from Dewey ("The phrase 'think for one's self' is a pleonasm. Unless one does it for one's self, it isn't thinking"), I introduced the problem I would be dealing with in this chapter, but attaching the problem to Dewey didn't make it more intellectually significant. I can only accomplish that by what I contribute to the topic. Even when we quote a definition from a dictionary or a population total from an almanac, we are offering a piece of information that demands to be explained, demands to be placed into a context of experience that makes the information meaningful. Quotations and paraphrases should, I believe, be seen as ways in which multiple voices are able to interact within a text. They become an amplification of the internal dialogue of thinking.

That, at least, is one answer to the question of the role of references and sources in writing and speech. It is not, however, the answer students are likely to surmise from those efforts to suppress plagiarism that stress precise citation of "reference materials." As long as citation of "the literature" is seen by students (and their teachers) as the source of intellectual weight, as the essence of their arguments, students will rightly conclude that the thinking of scholarship has been done for them and needs only to be quoted and cited.

This perspective is reinforced when we ask how it is that teaching students to paraphrase—the third common method of combating plagiarism— is supposed to deter academic dishonesty. What crime do students avoid when they paraphrase skillfully? Here is what an Internet site I quoted earlier says about the subject:

> Another activity that helps students develop their paraphrasing skills is to require them to write summaries without the text in front of them. Instructors can give the students short excerpts of Internet passages to read and summarize. As students read one another's summaries, they can determine whether "patchwriting" has occurred. If it appears that a summary matches the content of the article too closely, then students can be instructed on how to quote a paraphrased passage. (Hricko, 2004)

The danger, it seems, is that a student may quote passages without using quotation marks. The crime is that the student has borrowed the wording of an idea without asking for permission, which is (in the academic world, though not in the legal world) what proper citation and marking of the text amount to—permission to use the words. This illicit borrowing has, of course, another dimension in school writing. Students are evaluated on the quality of their writing, and when they try to pass off someone else's writing as their own, their theft is compounded by deceit, which complicates the process of comparing one student's work with another's and undermines the assumption of a just evaluation.

Another Internet source on the subject offers a notably different definition of *paraphrase*, arguing that it is not at all the same as *summary*, but arrives at a similar conclusion about the dangers of maladroit or dishonest paraphrasing. "Worst-case scenario," says this site written for students in a freshman composition class, "is that you get caught having read these people's work and using their ideas without giving them credit" (Merkner, 2004). Again the crime is that a student attempts to deceive by passing off someone else's work as her own. She can avoid the dishonesty (in part) through careful paraphrasing, which involves "Sentence-for-sentence recasting of author's ideas" along with "[c]areful, natural replacement of words w/synonyms and synonym phrases" (Merkner, 2004). If the wording is changed, quotation marks become unnecessary (though citation is still necessary). Skillful paraphrasing allows a student to use someone else's ideas without the intrusion of quotation marks. It looks as if it is the student's own work, and it can even be characterized as a kind of thinking, for it involves the restating of an original text. In the language of Bloom's *Taxonomy*, this is "translation" or "interpretation," the first two (of three) "types of comprehension behavior" associated with the second level of the taxonomy (Bloom et al., 1956, pp. 89–90).

The avoidance of quotation marks enabled by skillful paraphrasing may seem to be a small matter, but it suggests an answer to what is otherwise a puzzling question: Why paraphrase at all? Why not put quotation marks around every borrowing?

The disheartening answer is that everything is borrowed. Here, again, is the site advising students in the freshman composition class:

> Most (not all) academic writing is finding ways to repeat and restate what other people have said about an issue or topic. The key in academic writing is accepting this cold and brutal fact: someone else has already thought about the issues that you want to discuss before you have, and they have likely already made all of the "good points" about that issue. (Merkner, 2004)

Yes, it's true, says this Web site, there is nothing new under the sun, so that a student engaged in academic writing really has only three possibilities (as the title of the Web page indicates): She can summarize, paraphrase, or quote. What she can't do is think something new. It's already been thought.

This stunning assertion of what the Web site calls a "cold and brutal fact" carries with it the conclusion that thinking (in classrooms) is an illusion. There is no thinking for one's self. The only way to avoid turning in school papers that are simply a long string of quotations is to become skillful at paraphrasing, a skill that (Bloom notwithstanding) really does not require thinking. A computer program can translate text. Thinking, say the lessons on paraphrasing, is something done by other people. Originality is not an option.

Not surprisingly, this conclusion was rejected by Dewey decades before the Web site appeared. In the passage in which Dewey talks about the individuality of thinking, he also speaks about originality:

> If it is said in objection that pupils in school are not capable of any such originality, and hence must be confined to appropriating and reproducing things already known by the better informed, the reply is two-fold. (*i*) We are concerned with originality of attitude which is equivalent to the unforced response of one's own individuality, not with originality as measured by product. No one expects the young to make original discoveries of just the same facts and principles as are embodied in the sciences of nature and man.... (*ii*) In the normal process of becoming acquainted with subject matter already known to others, even young pupils react in unexpected ways. There is something fresh, something not capable of being fully anticipated by even the most experienced teacher, in the ways they go at the topic, and in the particular ways in which things strike them. (1916/1966, pp. 303–304)

Is originality, as Dewey argues, a genuine option in schoolwork? Can thinking for one's self exist within a classroom? Or is the non-thinking of "appropriating and reproducing," of "summary, paraphrase, and quotation," all that is possible?

ORIGINALITY OF ATTITUDE

The stakes are these: If a student believes that academic work is limited to "appropriating and reproducing," she can only conclude that the injunction to "think for yourself" is merely encouragement to behave and work hard. If there is no place for originality in academic work, the phrase "think for one's self" is empty of content.

Undoubtedly, there are those who do not find this troubling. There are those who would say that when Dewey talks about "appropriating and reproducing," he has accurately described the student's primary duties. The square root of 9 is 3; Thomas Jefferson was the third president of the United States; and there is no room for originality in such matters. Those who take this stance might even express skepticism about the call for "originality of attitude," saying that it is, rather, what Dewey calls "the product" that the school should be concerned with, not some hypothetical attitude.

But if we wish to strive against those conditions of schooling that encourage non-thinking, we must make meaningful the concept of thinking for one's self. What would Dewey's "originality of attitude" amount to in school-work? What would it look like in practice? To work toward an answer to these questions, I want to begin with a quite different question, one that may seem at first completely unconnected to the idea of thinking for one's self but will lead to a deeper understanding of that aim. The question is this: How does learning make us good?

This question can be seen as a version of the search for a relationship between knowledge and virtue, though I presume (in the way I phrase the question) more certainty than the history of the issue in Western philosophy warrants. Plato portrays Socrates both asserting a link between knowledge and virtue and being forced to confess that he cannot confirm such a link. Many modern philosophers, from Immanuel Kant to the positivists of the 20th century, questioned the possibility of a link between knowledge and virtue, as they sought to prove (or assumed) a strict boundary between fact and value, truth and practical judgment.

Yet schooling has been, and continues to be, planned and conducted along lines that imply that learning does in fact make us good. Students have long been brought into contact with subject matter that was justified not because it trained them in a practical skill, but because it was supposed to make them "good citizens" or "well rounded" or simply "educated." This is why universities require students to take "general education" courses, why high-school students read Shakespeare's plays, why elementary schools adopt "character education" programs. Debates continue, of course, about the merits of such curricula and about what precisely should be included in order that students will learn what we want them to learn, but these debates do not question the underlying assumption: the right kind of learning makes us good.

But how does that work? Is it the search itself that improves us (as Plato seems to imply in his dialogue *Meno*), or do only certain lessons, certain pieces of information, improve us? Here are some test cases. Which of them are morally imbued? Which are the sorts of lessons or school activities that will make students better people?

1. Home plate and the three bases of a standard baseball diamond form a square. The distance from home plate to first base is 90 feet. How

large is the area enclosed by home plate and the three bases? Suppose you made a new baseball diamond. The path from home to second base on the original (standard) diamond will now be used as the path from home to first base on your new diamond, with new second and third bases positioned to create a new square. How much bigger is the area enclosed by home plate and the three bases of the new diamond than the area enclosed by home plate and the three bases of the original diamond?

2. Students are required to memorize the order of the planets in the solar system, along with their diameters, their average distances from the sun, and their periodic revolutions.

3. Students will read and discuss Wordsworth's "Ode: Intimations of Immortality from Recollections of Early Childhood," from which the following stanza is excerpted:

> Our birth is but a sleep and a forgetting:
> The Soul that rises with us, our life's Star,
>   Hath had elsewhere its setting,
>   And cometh from afar:
>   Not in entire forgetfulness,
>   And not in utter nakedness,
> But trailing clouds of glory do we come
>   From God, who is our home:
> Heaven lies about us in our infancy!
> Shades of the prison-house begin to close
>   Upon the growing Boy,
>   But he
> Beholds the light, and whence it flows,
>   He sees it in his joy;
> The Youth, who daily farther from the east
>   Must travel, still is Nature's Priest,
>   And by the vision splendid
>   Is on his way attended;
> At length the Man perceives it die away,
> And fade into the light of common day.

I have received quite a range of responses from teachers and teacher educators to these test cases. The third test case—discussing Wordsworth's "Ode"—has been the case most consistently seen as morally imbued. Respondents have noted that the poem is concerned with God and the soul and that these religious terms imply moral messages, though some respondents have worried that "some children" will find the poem does not fit their "faith" and that the clash will undercut the potential for moral significance. Other respondents have focused on the instructional strategy—discussion—and have seen in this form of instruction intimations that students are reflecting and thinking rather than "memorizing." The distinction between reflection and memorization is significant, respondents have argued, because thinking about the poem is necessary for it to have any moral effect. However, some respondents have rejected the possibility of moral effect from the activity of discussing Wordsworth's "Ode." One respondent said simply that he found poetry (both in general and in this instance) so cold, formal, and boring that he doubted any children could be affected in any way by it.

The second test case—memorizing data about the planets—has been the one in which respondents are least likely to find moral significance. Some respondents have dismissed it simply because it is limited to memorization. On one occasion this assertion sparked discussion about other things that are memorized, such as the Lord's Prayer, and respondents concluded that sometimes memorizing might have moral significance, but not if "meaning is missing" in the recitation of what is memorized. This was taken as further evidence that the second test case is not morally imbued, because data about the planets were not seen as meaningful. As one respondent expressed it, if the subject matter caused her to ask, "What is my role in the universe?" it would be a meaningful and morally significant topic, but as it was, it was "just numbers." Another respondent suggested that this activity might actually have "immoral significance." Her position was that this sort of memorizing perpetuates a deeply flawed notion of education and therefore teaches children a bad lesson.

The first test case—the baseball diamond math problem—has been the one respondents disagreed about most. Some have dismissed the possibility of moral significance because the activity "doesn't touch values" and has nothing to do with "your own personal belief system." Others (typically math teachers) have argued that solving the problem requires persistence and planning and that therefore the activity teaches desirable traits. Some have said that "general knowledge makes you who you are" and that we never know "what could be moral help to someone else." One respondent rejected the possibility of moral significance because of her antipathy for mathematics, and another wondered if there was something perverse or deceitful involved in changing the dimensions of a baseball diamond. We need to ask, he said, what effect this will have on the game.

In sum, respondents have said in response to the question about moral significance in the test cases, "It depends."

This, it seems to me, is a good beginning, but the sentence needs to be completed. On what does the possibility of moral significance depend? The answer, of course, is that it depends on how people think about these activities. Without the input of students, the subject matter of the test cases is inert, an assertion that takes on even more meaning when the sources of the cases are examined.

The math problem is probably recognizable as an updated version of the geometry lesson that Socrates teaches to the slave in Plato's *Meno* (82b–85b). I discussed this passage in Chapter 2, but I want to look at it now from a somewhat different perspective. Instructed by his master to answer some questions, the slave begins confidently because the questions that Socrates asks are easy: Is this a square? Are the sides equal? Could it be bigger or smaller than it is? Then Socrates asks how long a side he would have to draw to make a square twice as big as the one he has drawn (with sides of 2 feet and an area of 4 one-unit blocks). The slave says the side will have to be twice as long (or 4 feet). It's at this point that the questions begin to become more difficult because the slave sees (after some more of Socrates' questions) that making the side twice as long makes the square four times as big. Obviously, the side will have to be shorter. The slave concludes that the side must therefore be 3 feet, but after more questions, he sees that even this is too long a side. It makes a square with 9 one-unit blocks in it, and he has been asked to make a square with 8 one-unit blocks (twice the original). The slave now faces a dilemma: He is looking for a number bigger than 2 and smaller than 3, and in his mathematics there are no fractions. He has been instructed by his master to answer some questions, and there is no answer to this question. When he recognizes and confesses his ignorance—"By Zeus, Socrates, I do not know"—he expresses what this geometry problem has come to mean to him. Shapes in the sand, though they seem so clear and simple, hold mysteries.

The second test case—memorizing information about the planets—comes from the memoir of Emma Hart Willard. As a young girl, she was given the opportunity of going to school. She refused it at first, but soon decided that she did want to attend the classes and study from the books she saw her sister studying from. This meant that she would have to catch up with the rest of class. "Mr. Miner," she says, "was to hear me recite by myself until I overtook the class, in which there were a dozen fine girls, including my elder sister" (Willard, in Cohen & Scheer, 1997, p. 43). She tells proudly how she memorized so much of Webster's Grammar that Mr. Miner's questions "went on and on" until he decided he would postpone the remainder of the recitation for the following day. The same thing happened with her geography lesson:

> That hard chapter on the planets, with their diameters, distances, and periodic revolutions, was among the first of Morse's *Geography*. The evening I wished to learn it, my sister Lydia had a party. The house was full of bustle, and above all rose the song-singing, which always fascinated me. The moon was at the full, and snow was on the ground. I wrapt my cloak around me, and out of doors of a cold winter evening, seated on a horseblock, I learned that lesson. Lessons so learnt are not easily forgotten. (Willard, in Cohen & Scheer, 1997, p. 43)

Willard doesn't speak in her memoir about the numbers meaning anything to her beyond the pride she took in memorizing them. Would it matter if she were memorizing data about another planetary system somewhere else in the galaxy? Probably not. She was mostly interested in showing how much "hard" material she could master.

The abstractness of the information (she doesn't seem to think about the planets being visible in the sky above her) defines accomplishment differently from the way that Socrates' geometry problem defines it. There is no deeper understanding that introspection can reveal; there are only more numbers.

But when Willard says that she mastered those numbers on that cold winter night, she expresses what this subject matter meant to her: It was a way to demonstrate intellectual competence, a way to show that a mere girl could master the cosmos as the scholars had defined it.

The third test case—discussing William Wordsworth's "Ode"—comes from Elizabeth Palmer Peabody's (1836/1969) description of Bronson Alcott's Temple School. Alcott was teaching a group of children who ranged in age from about 4 years to 12 years. He had been talking to them about what "birth" means, when he began reading Wordsworth's poem. He stopped periodically to discuss the meaning of the poem, and after reading the line, "Our birth is but a sleep, and a forgetting," he stopped again, Peabody tells us,

> and asked how that was? After a pause, one of the most intelligent boys, eight years old, said he could not imagine. The two oldest girls said, they understood it, but could not explain it in words. (p. 110)

A little boy (Peabody does not tell us how young he was) then held up his hand and said he thought he knew what it meant.

> Why, you know, said he very deliberately, that, for all that our life seems so long to us, it is a very short time to God; and so when we die it seems all a sleep to God. . . . Why, you know, said he, *God knows us, but we don't.* (p. 110)

With these words, the boy expresses his dawning realization that his own life and experience are described in Wordsworth's poem. When he talks about what the poem, and in particular this one line from the poem, means to him, he is not offering an interpretation in which he keeps the poem at arm's length and discusses it with disinterest. He speaks, in a sense, from inside the poem. Am I claiming, then, that the boy's response is individual because he says something that neither Alcott nor Peabody nor any other critic of Wordsworth's poetry had yet realized? No, the boy's response is probably not a major step in the history of literary criticism. But it is his response; even though it is helped along by the questions and urgings of Alcott and Peabody, it is his response.

The day after this lesson, Peabody writes,

> Mr. Alcott talked a little with the little commentator of yesterday, commending him for his writing, and especially because he had been rather indocile, not through opposition, but from a sort of obstinate clinging to his own inward thoughts. (p. 111)

Originality of attitude probably often looks like indocility, like an obstinate clinging to one's own inward thoughts, but originality of attitude is not a matter of stubbornness, nor is individuality a matter of isolation. Alcott's young student is individual in his thinking because Wordsworth's poem has become part of the boy, part of how he now sees himself. He has opened himself to Wordsworth's intimations of immortality and made himself a larger being. This is, I suspect, what Martin Heidegger has in mind when he speaks of being "open to thoughts which thinkers before . . . have thought." Without this openness, says Martin Heidegger, we will "suffer from constipated originality." We will worry about creating something original rather than holding "on to what is to be thought" (1968, p. 95).

Curricular material—whether it is figures drawn in the sand or the constructions of a graphing calculator, whether it is words and numbers on a page or images on a computer screen—is inert until it is enlivened by a student. What brings it to life is the activity of a student beginning to articulate what it means to know this thing. This sort of thinking might be called metacognitive, but that suggests I am concerned with looking at how these students look at their own thinking. Instead, I am more concerned with how they think about what it means for them as individual human beings to know geometry, the stars, or eternity. Until the slave can articulate that learning geometry means recognizing and admitting that he does not know (but that finding out is possible), until Willard can articulate that learning the solar system means using her female brain to master the abstractions of science, until the little boy can articulate that learning Wordsworth means finding the eternal within himself—until students can talk about what it means to themselves to know this thing—curriculum cannot become part of character nor become meaningful, because it remains external to the learner.

My answer to the question "How does learning make us good?" is that when we take the first step toward finding meaning in curricular material, we start by seeing curriculum as part of our character, as part of who we are or who we would like to become. This is what I believe Dewey means by "originality of attitude." This attitude is not void of content, but neither is it the end of knowing. It is the starting point. It is where thinking begins.

FINDING OURSELVES

I began this chapter by asking how the individuality of thinking could ever have been in doubt such that Dewey would need to say that all thinking is thinking for one's self. Why should this truism need to be made explicit?

The answer, it seems, is that when we become more fully aware of what it means to say that thinking is an individual matter, we find once again that our grasp weakens and that this experience we call "thinking" begins to elude our attempts to define, control, and understand it. We think to solve problems, but when we take a problem as our own, thinking does not settle anything; it unsettles. To take a problem as our own is to embrace uncertainty. To take a problem as our own is to be changed in unpredictable ways. Non-thinking is safer.

If thinking is our own, surely we can be confident of its existence and importance. But then the individuality of thinking also points toward the duality of the two-in-one and the "withdrawal-and-return" that characterizes internal dialogue, and we begin to wonder if thinking is really anything at all. In the classroom it is conclusions that matter. Thinking is too ephemeral, too individual, and non-thinking is preferable.

Finally, the individuality of thinking calls for originality, but in academic speaking and writing everything that we would say has (we fear) already been said. We teach students that originality is an illusion created by reshuffling other people's words. We teach them that non-thinking is all that they can do.

And yet reflection on thinking as an "individual matter" also reveals that, by the exercise of originality of attitude, thinking for one's self is possible. Students do not need to contribute to the development of a field of study in order to exercise originality. The student who finds herself in the curriculum exercises originality of attitude and takes the first essential step toward thinking. Unfortunately, students too often find themselves outside the curriculum. Asked "What does this curriculum mean to you?" their answer is "Nothing." And as long as that is their answer, non-thinking will prevail.

Epilogue

When the National Weather Service warns the people living in a coastal area about an impending hurricane, no one supposes that the residents will be able to stop or deflect the storm. But their inability to change the weather doesn't mean that the warning is pointless or that there is nothing for the people to do. They are able to board up windows or stock up on fresh water or even to leave town. They cannot prevent the progress of the hurricane, but they can, to some extent, change its effects.

This book—my description of some of the causes of non-thinking—is in some ways like the National Weather Service warning. I have argued that commonplaces of teaching and learning—inevitable conditions of education, not problems to be solved—encourage non-thinking. If my argument that teaching is enmeshed in the paradoxes of defining, telling, and believing is well founded, there can be no prescription for schooling that removes the threat of non-thinking. The hurricane will come regardless of what the residents do.

We recognize the tendency of instruction—because it is segmented into discrete disciplines—to teach defined procedures and to neglect the thinking that occurs between the boundaries of disciplines. So we determine to improve our curricula by making them more interdisciplinary and focusing on "higher-order thinking." Have we removed the concept of a "discipline" from schooling? No, we have only created new disciplines.

We recognize the tendency of teachers—because they tell students things—to create the impression on their students that thinking is unnecessary because their teacher will tell them what they need to know. So we determine to improve teaching by telling students that they must draw their own conclusions about the materials we present to them. Have we removed "telling" from schooling? No, we have only declared that the materials— books, videos, manipulatives—will do our telling for us.

We recognize the tendency of students—because of their longing for cognitive closure—to believe things and thereby put an end to thinking. So we determine to improve their experience by teaching them to distinguish between facts and opinions and by having them think for themselves. Have we removed "believing" from schooling? No, we have only made it irrelevant to the business of the classroom.

The hurricane will come regardless of what the residents do. But even if we cannot stop non-thinking in its tracks, even if we cannot excise it from school life, we are still able to act in ways that diminish its effects.

We can, from the start, acknowledge that we do not possess the secret of thinking, that our best definitions of *thinking* are really characterizations of what thinking is not. This is a difficult acknowledgement to make not only because we teachers espouse thinking as our lifelong partner but also because of the fragility of our expertise in an era of school bashing. When politicians routinely demonstrate their "education" credentials by asserting the incompetence of teachers and the failure of schools, a confession of ignorance about the nature of thinking sounds unconscionable. If we cannot say what thinking is, how can we call ourselves teachers?

The answer to this question lies in our ability to argue persuasively that it is more important for a teacher to be alert to occurrences of non-thinking than it is for her to guide her students toward a watered-down version of thinking. Teachers should be leery of shortcuts to thinking—definitions that are too precise, verbs that are magically supposed to induce student thought, question-starters that guarantee the activation of "higher mental processes," activities that are sure to engage all of a student's "intelligences."

Teachers should be alert for signs that they themselves or their students have lapsed into the "academic" characterization of thinking. They should feel the incongruity when thinking becomes a purely mental activity, isolated from life; when it loses its affective dimensions; when it is associated too narrowly with words and numbers; when it is associated too narrowly with answering questions; when it is separated both from the practical and the sublime; when it becomes the tool of the disciplines, forever external to the student.

Teachers should monitor their own telling, alert for the possibility that they are imposing meaning, alert too for the possibility that they allow story to become meaningless by opening it to any meaning. They should remember that every instance of telling calls for a surrender to the text, a surrender that limits thinking even as the text expands the possibilities of thinking.

Teachers should be alert for those times when their instincts to treat students fairly and to speak about things that matter reduce the opportunities for students to respond to what they are told. A teacher should shrink back from holding students accountable only for what she can tell them; even in her search for truth, she should steer clear of hewing to the objectively true.

Teachers should be alert for signs that their students look only for truth and ignore meaning. They should be ready to abort activities that encourage students to speak of "facts" and "opinions" as if these words describe statements rather than rhetorical intentions.

Teachers should be alert to the tendency to diminish the importance of thinking in favor of action. They should be on their guard against supposing that thinking settles matters—rather than unsettling thinkers. They should be on their guard against the insidious fear that originality is impossible.

Each of these admonitions to be alert is a call for action, but cobbling them together into a prescription for action would be a mistake. It would be just another instance of non-thinking. These admonitions are not a list or schedule of things for the teacher to do; they are a voice in her ear that says simply, "Beware."

My warning about the onslaught of non-thinking lacks the human drama and acute peril carried by a hurricane warning, and I suspect that the subtlety and pervasiveness of the danger explain why we tend not to take it seriously, even though we know our public discourse is awash in nonsense and non-thinking. Genuine problems are raised (dissatisfaction with schools, economic decline, terror and war, environmental degradation), and slogans are intoned ("hold students to standards," "grow jobs," "stand firm against the threat," "protect the environment responsibly"). Daily we see the spectacle of well-meaning leaders—in government, in business, in education—responding to the living problems of our world as if the answers could be copied out of a book. The lessons of non-thinking learned in school become the template for "thinking" in the rest of life.

Some people are not bothered by this institutionalization of non-thinking, because they find the model of non-thinking to be a suitable goal for schools. They say there are many things we do not want our children to think about. Some of these things are odious—pornography, hateful ideologies, the creation and use of tools of violence. And there are other things (they say) that we do not need to avoid but yet are best "learned" through "non-thinking" because we know what we want our children to think about them—the inalienable rights of democracy, the fairness of capitalism, the evils of drug abuse, the benefits of a good education, the role of the United States in world history. The task of schools is precisely (they say) to be sure that children do not think about that which is despicable and that they do not think wrongly about that which is certain.

It is even argued that non-thinking is a suitable goal for schools because not everyone is capable of thinking.

Each of these defenses of non-thinking is made in schools every day even though our children live in a world in which any image, any imaginable claim, and every conceivable piece of information is immediately available at the nearest computer terminal. The legends of ancient worlds were crafted in the evanescent breath of itinerant storytellers, but our legends are fixed in hard-edged print on glowing computer screens. How will our children, so carefully schooled in the lessons of non-thinking, wield their infinite knowledge?

References

Adler, M. J. (1977). Labor, leisure, and liberal education. In *Reforming education: The opening of the American mind* (pp. 93–113). New York: Macmillan. (Original work published 1951)

Anagnostopolous, D. (2005). Testing, tests, and classrooms texts. *Journal of Curriculum Studies 37*(1), 35–63.

Anderson, L. W., & Sosniak, L. A. (Eds.). (1994). *Bloom's taxonomy: A 40-year retrospective. Ninety-third yearbook of the National Society for the Study of Education. Part II.* Chicago: National Society for the Study of Education.

Apol, L. (2002). The power of text: What a 19th century periodical taught me about reading and the reader's response. *Journal of Children's Literature, 28*(1), 53–60.

Arendt, H. (1978). *The life of the mind: Vol. 1. Thinking.* New York: Harcourt Brace Jovanovich.

Aristotle. (1984). *The complete works of Aristotle.* (Revised Oxford Translation in two volumes). J. Barnes (Ed.). Princeton: Princeton University Press.

Armstrong, T. (2000). Multiple intelligences. Retrieved October 2, 2003, from http://thomasarmstrong.com/multiple_intelligences.htm.

Auden, W. H. (1958). *Selected poetry of W. H. Auden.* New York: Random House.

Auden, W. H. (1960). *Homage to Clio.* New York: Random House.

Bartlett, F. C. (1958). *Thinking: An experimental and social study.* New York: Basic Books.

Bennett, W. (1993). *The book of virtues.* New York: Simon & Schuster.

Bloom, B. S. (1994). Reflections on the development and use of the taxonomy. In *Bloom's taxonomy: A 40-year retrospective. Ninety-third yearbook of the National Society for the Study of Education. Part II,* L. W. Anderson & L. A. Sosniak (Eds.) (pp. 1–8). Chicago: National Society for the Study of Education.

Bloom, B. S., Engelhart, M. D., Furst, E. J., Hill, W. H., & Krathwohl, D. R. (1956). *Taxonomy of educational objectives: The classification of educational goals (Handbook 1: Cognitive domain).* New York: David McKay.

Boostrom, R. (1997). Teaching by the numbers. In N. C. Burbules & D. T. Hansen (Eds.), *Teaching and its predicaments,* (pp. 45–64). Boulder, CO: Westview Press.

Booth, W. C. (1961). *The rhetoric of fiction*. Chicago: University of Chicago Press.

Changeux, J.-P., & Ricoeur, P. (2000). *What makes us think? A neuroscientist and a philosopher argue about ethics, human nature, and the brain*. Princeton: Princeton University Press.

Ciardi, J. (1959). *How does a poem mean? Part III of an introduction to literature*. Cambridge, MA: Riverside Press.

Cohen, R. M., & Scheer, S. (Eds.). (1997). *The work of teachers in America: A social history through stories*. Mahwah, NJ: Erlbaum.

Coles, R. (1989). *The call of stories*. Boston: Houghton-Mifflin.

Cunningham, G. K. (2002). The culture of progressive education and the culture of traditionalists. Retrieved February 11, 2004, from http://www.educationnews. org/culture_of_progressive_education.htm.

Cunningham, G. K. (2003). Can education schools be saved? Speech at American Enterprise Institute conference, June 9, 2003, Washington, D.C. Retrieved February 11, 2004, from http://www.aei.org/news/newsID.17804/news_detail.asp.

Davidson, T. (1969). *Aristotle and ancient educational ideals*. New York: Burt Franklin. (Original work published 1892)

Dement, W. C., & Vaughan, C. (1999). *The promise of sleep: A pioneer in sleep medicine explores the vital connection between health, happiness, and a good night's sleep*. New York: Dell.

Dewey, J. (1966). *Democracy and education*. New York: Macmillan. (Original work published 1916)

Dewey, J. (1977). The significance of the problem of knowledge. In David Sidorksy (Ed.), *John Dewey: The essential writings*, (pp. 53–69) New York: Harper Torchbooks. (Original work published 1897)

Dewey, J. (1980). *Art as experience*. New York: Perigee Books. (Original work published 1934)

Dewey, J. (1990). *The school and society/The child and the curriculum*. Chicago: University of Chicago Press. (Original work published 1902)

Dewey, J. (1991). *How we think*. Buffalo, NY: Prometheus Books. (Original work published 1910)

Dewey, J. (1998b). The pattern of inquiry. In L. A. Hickman & T. M. Alexander (Eds.), *The essential Dewey: Vol. 2. Ethics, logic, psychology* (pp. 169–179). Bloomington: Indiana University Press. (Original work published 1938)

Dewey, J. (1998c). The problem of logical subject matter. In L. A. Hickman & T. M. Alexander (Eds.), *The essential Dewey: Vol. 2. Ethics, logic, psychology* (pp. 157–168). Bloomington: Indiana University Press. (Original work published 1938)

Dewey, J. (1998d). The problem of truth. In L. A. Hickman & T. M. Alexander (Eds.), *The essential Dewey: Vol. 2. Ethics, logic, psychology* (pp. 101–130). Bloomington: Indiana University Press. (Original work published 1911)

Dickens, C. (1981). *Hard times*. New York: Bantam Books. (Original work published 1854)

Doyle, W., & Carter, K. (2003). Narrative and learning to teach: Implications for teacher-education curriculum. *Journal of Curriculum Studies, 35*(2), 129–137.

Du Bois, W. E. B. (1990). *The souls of Black folk.* New York: Vintage Books. (Original work published 1903)

Eliot, G. (1964). *Middlemarch.* New York: New American Library. (Original work published 1872)

Fish, S. (1980). *Is there a text in this class? The authority of interpretive communities.* Cambridge, MA: Harvard University Press.

Fleener, M. J., Carter, A., & Reeder, S. (2004). Language games in the mathematics classroom: Teaching a way of life. *Journal of Curriculum Studies, 36*(4), 445–468.

Fowler, B. (1996). Bloom's taxonomy and critical thinking. Critical Thinking Across the Curriculum Project. Retrieved September 10, 2003, from http://kcmetro.cc.mo.us/longview/ctac/blooms.htm.

Fried, R. L. (1996). *The passionate teacher: A practical guide.* Boston: Beacon Press.

Frost, R. (1928). *West-running brook.* New York: Henry Holt.

Gardner, H. (1999a). Are there additional intelligences? The case for naturalist, spiritual, and existential intelligences. In J. Kane (Ed.), *Education, information, and transformation: Essays on learning and thinking* (pp. 111–131). Upper Saddle River, NJ: Prentice-Hall.

Gardner, H. (1999b). *Intelligence reframed: Multiple intelligences for the 21st century.* New York: Basic Books.

Goodman, N. (1978). *Ways of worldmaking.* Indianapolis, IN: Hackett.

Gwynn, A. (1926). *Roman education: From Cicero to Quintilian.* Oxford: Clarendon Press.

Heidegger, M. (1968). *What is called thinking.* (J. Glenn Gray, Trans.). New York: Harper & Row.

Hirsch, E. D., Jr. (1987). *Cultural literacy: What every american needs to know.* Boston, MA: Houghton Mifflin.

Hirsch, E. D., Jr. (Ed.). (1992). *What your fourth grader needs to know: Fundamentals of a good fourth-grade education.* New York: Doubleday.

Hirsch, E. D., Kett, J. F., & Trefil, J. (2002). *The New Dictionary of Cultural Literacy.* Boston, MA: Houghton Mifflin.

Hricko, M. (2004). Internet plagiarism: Strategies to deter academic misconduct. Retrieved January 20, 2004, from http://www.mtsu.edu/~itconf/proceed98/mhricko.html.

Irwin, W., Conrad, M. T., & Skoble, A. (Eds.). (2001). *The Simpsons and philosophy: The d'oh! of Homer.* Chicago: Open Court.

Jackson, P. W. (1986). *The practice of teaching.* New York: Teachers College Press.

Jackson, P. W., Boostrom, R., & Hansen, D. T. (1993). *The moral life of schools.* San Francisco: Jossey-Bass.

Kestenbaum, V. (2002). *The grace and the severity of the ideal.* Chicago: University of Chicago Press.

Klein, P. D. (2003). Rethinking the multiplicity of cognitive resources and curricular representations: Alternatives to "learning styles" and "multiple intelligences." *Journal of Curriculum Studies, 35*(1), 45–81.

Krumme, G. (1995). Major categories in the taxonomy of educational objectives

(Bloom 1956). Retrieved September 10, 2003, from http://faculty.washington.edu/krumme/guides/bloom.html.

Lampert, M. (2001). *Teaching problems and the problems of teaching*. New Haven: Yale University Press.

Locke, J. (1975). *An essay concerning human understanding*. Oxford: Oxford University Press. (Original work published 1700)

Marrou, H. I. (1964). *A history of education in antiquity*. (George Lamb, Trans.). New York: Mentor.

McKenzie, W. (1999). It's not how smart you are—it's how you are smart. Retrieved October 2, 2003, from http://surfaquarium.com/MI/mi.htm.

McPeck, J. E. (1990). *Teaching critical thinking: Dialogue and dialectic*. New York: Routledge.

Merkner, C. (2004). Summary, paraphrase, quotation. Retrieved January 30, 2004, from http://clem.mscd.edu/~merkner/ENG1020/sumparquo.htm.

Murdoch, I. (1993). *Metaphysics as a guide to morals*. London: Penguin Books.

National Center for Education Statistics. (2004). Internet access in U.S. public schools and classrooms: 1994–2001. Retrieved January 22, 2004, from http://nces.ed.gov/pubs2002/internet.

Newbigin, L. (1989). *The gospel in a pluralist society*. Grand Rapids, MI: William B. Eerdmans.

Noddings, N. (1992). *The challenge to care in schools: An alternative approach to education*. New York: Teachers College Press.

Nussbaum, M. C. (1997). *Cultivating humanity: A classical defense of reform in liberal education*. Cambridge, MA: Harvard University Press.

Peabody, E. P. (1969). *Record of a school*. New York: Arno Press and the New York Times. (Original work published 1836)

Phillips, D. C. (Ed). (2000). *Constructivism in education: Opinions and second opinions on controversial issues* (Ninety-ninth yearbook of the National Society for the Study of Education, Part I). Chicago: University of Chicago Press.

Plagiarism Detection—YAP. (2004). Retrieved January 20, 2004, from http://www.cs.usyd.edu.au/~michaelw/YAP.html.

Plagiarism.org. (2004). *Plagiarism today*. Retrieved January 20, 2004, from http://www.plagiarism.org/plagiarism.html.

Plato. (1961). *The collected dialogues of Plato, including the letters*. (E. Hamilton and H. Cairns, Eds.). Princeton: Princeton University Press.

Plato. (1997). *Complete works*. (J. M. Cooper, Ed.). Indianapolis, IN: Hackett.

Pope, D. (2001). *"Doing school": How we are creating a generation of stressed out, materialistic, and miseducated students*. New Haven: Yale University Press.

Rait, R. (1912). *Life in the medieval university*. Cambridge: Cambridge University Press.

Resnick, L. B. (1987). *Education and learning to think*. Washington, DC: National Academy Press.

Rosenblatt, L. (1978). *The reader, the text, the poem: The transactional theory of the literary work*. Carbondale, IL: Southern Illinois University Press.

Russell, B. (1967). Dewey's new *Logic*. In *The basic writings of Bertrand Russell*. New York: Simon & Schuster. (Original work published 1939)

Schick, T., Jr., & Vaughn, L. (2002). *How to think about weird things: Critical thinking for a new age* (3rd ed.). Boston, MA: McGraw-Hill.

Scholes, R. (2001). *The crafty reader*. New Haven, CN: Yale University Press.

Searle, J. R. (1980). Minds, brains, and programs. *Behavioral and Brain Sciences, 3*, 417–424.

Searle, J. R. (1998). *Mind, language, and society: Philosophy in the real world*. New York: Basic Books.

Shook, J. R. (2000). *Dewey's empirical theory of knowledge and reality*. Nashville, TN: Vanderbilt University Press.

Simon, K. G. (2001). *Moral questions in the classroom: How to get kids to think deeply about real life and their schoolwork*. New Haven, CT: Yale University Press.

Stahl, W. H. (1971). *The quadrivium of Martianus Capella: Latin traditions in the mathematical sciences: 50 B.C.–A.D. 1250*. In W. H. Stahl & R. Johnson (with E. L. Burge), *Martianus Capella and the seven liberal arts* (Vol. 1, pp. 1–79). New York: Columbia University Press.

Stengel, B. S. (2001). Making use of the method of intelligence. *Educational Theory, 51*(1), 109–125.

Sternberg, R. J. (2003). What is an "expert student"? *Educational Researcher, 32*(8), 5–9.

Terhart, E. (2003). Constructivism and teaching: A new paradigm in general didactics. *Journal of Curriculum Studies, 35*(1): 25–44.

Thurber, J. (1964). The Macbeth murder mystery. In *The Thurber carnival*, (pp. 60–63). New York: Dell. (Original work published 1938)

Toynbee, A. (1962). *A study of history: Vol. 3. The growths of civilizations*. New York: Oxford University Press.

Wagner, D. L. (1983). *The seven liberal arts in the Middle Ages*. Bloomington: Indiana University Press.

Index

A

Abelard, Pierre, 53, 70
Abstractions, and beliefs, 107–8
Accountability, 24, 96, 104, 140–41, 157
Acts, and content of stories, 68
Adams, John (composer), 65–66
Adler, M. J., 37, 40
Adventurous thinking, 13, 18
Affective aspect, 20, 52, 54, 156
Alcott, Bronson, 152–53
American Educational Research Association, 15
"American woman" (fictional character), 58–60, 70–71, 76–77
Anagnostopoulos, Dorothea, 90–94, 99
Analysis, 21, 22–24, 25, 26
Anderson, L. W., 19–20
Anderson, R. C., 85
Any-thing, 64
Apol, Laura, 77–79
Application, 21, 23–24, 25
Archimedes, 47
Architecture, and seven liberal arts, 44
Arendt, Hannah, 110, 116, 137, 138, 139
Aristotle, 11, 37, 49, 109
Arithmetic and calculation, 44, 45, 53. *See also* Mathematics
Armstrong, T., 30

Arts
　frivolous, 46
　liberal, 39, 43–47, 52, 53, 54
　manual, 46
　that teach virtue, 46
Assessment, 2, 31–32, 37, 95. *See also* Evaluation; Testing
Association for General and Liberal Studies, 15
Astronomy, 44, 45, 49, 53, 117
Astrophysics, 118
Attitude, originality of, 147–53, 154, 157
Auden, W. H., 101
Augustine, Saint, 54

B

Bach, Johann Sebastian, 66
"The Ballad of the Landlord" (Hughes), 62, 63, 70
Bartlett, Frederick Charles, 11, 12–13, 25
Baseball diamond math problem, 148–49, 150, 151
Batman story, 98–99
"Being smart," 111–12
Believing
　and categories of beliefs, 108
　as end of thinking, 108
　overview of, 107–9

About the Author

In the last 30 years, Robert Boostrom has worked as a high school teacher (English, social studies, and reading), textbook editor and writer, occasional home-schooling parent, and (since receiving a Ph.D. at the University of Chicago) associate professor of education at the University of Southern Indiana. With Philip Jackson and David Hansen, he is co-author of *The Moral Life of Schools*. Since 1997, he has been the U.S. Editor for the *Journal of Curriculum Studies*. He continues to believe that teaching and learning make life worth living.

FE